AT FOUR O'CLOCK IN THE AFTERNOON

GULEEG HAROIAN, née TOOMASIAN

Translated by Rose D. Guerin, PhD
Edited by Gil Harootunian, PhD
Afterword by Rebecca Jinks

TWO ORAL HISTORIES

BONES AND BODIES, WE HAD TO WALK OVER THEM

EVA HIGHTAIAN (née HAROIAN)

Edited by Gil Harootunian, PhD
Afterword by Rebecca Jinks

TADEM PRESS
FRESNO, CALIFORNIA

Tadem Press

www.tadempress.com

Printed in the United States of America

Library of Congress Cataloging-in-Publication data

Names: Haroian, Guleeg, 1886-1981, author. | Hightaian, Eva, 1905-1996,
                author. | Guerin, Rose D.,1923-2002, translator. | Harootunian,
                Gillisann, 1957- editor. | Jinks, Rebecca, writer of afterword.

Title: At four o'clock in the afternoon ..." / by Guleeg Haroian, née Toomasian
                ; translated by Rose D. Guerin, PhD (née Haroian) ; edited by Gil
                Harootunian, PhD (née Guerin) and: Bones and bodies, we had to
                walk over them / by Eva Hightaian (née Haroian) ; edited by Gil
                Harootunian ; Afterword: Genocidal captivity and absorption in
                comparative context by Dr. Rebecca Jinks.

Other titles: Bones and bodies, we had to walk over them. | Genocidal captivity and
                absorption in comparative context.

Description: Fresno, California : Tadem Press, [2023] | Includes bibliographical
                references and index.

Identifiers: ISBN: 978-1-7375558-2-7 (hardcover) | 978-1-7375558-3-4 (e-book) |
                LCCN: 2023903563

Subjects: LCSH: Haroian, Guleeg, 1886-1981. | Hightaian, Eva, 1905-1996.
                | World War, 1914-1918— Personal narratives, Armenian. | World
                War, 1914-1918—Atrocities—Personal narratives, Armenian. |
                Armenian Genocide, 1915-1923—Personal narratives. | Armenian
                massacres, 1894-1896—Personal narratives. | Armenian Genocide
                survivors—Turkey—History. | Armenians—Turkey—Social life and
                customs—1915-1923. | World War, 1914-1918— Deportations from
                Turkey. | Forced marriage—Turkey—1915-1923. | World War, 1914-
                1918 —Forced removal of civilians—Turkey. | Human trafficking—
                Turkey—1915-1923. | Orphans— Turkey—History—1915-1923. |
                BISAC: BIOGRAPHY & AUTOBIOGRAPHY / Personal Memoirs.
                | BIOGRAPHY & AUTOBIOGRAPHY / Survival. | HISTORY
                / Middle East / Turkey & Ottoman Empire. | BIOGRAPHY &
                AUTOBIOGRAPHY / Women.

Classification: LCC: DS195.5 .H37 2023 | DDC: 956.6/2015—dc23

To

[Great-Great-Grandmother] Vartouhi ("Rose") Der Aharonian
Murdered, 1895 Great Massacre, thrown down wheat well

[Great-Grandmother] Vartouhi ("Rose") Toomasian, née Der Aharonian
Deported, killed with group slaughtered outside village with stones, knives, etc., 1915

[Grandmother] Guleeg ("Rose") Haroian, née Toomasian, b. 1885
Gang raped, transferred to Muslim household 1915, self-rescued 1919

[Aunt] Mary Haroian, b. 1904
Deported 1915, transferred to Muslim household, and abused, abandoned, and perished 1918

[Aunt] Eva Hightaian, née Haroian, b. 1906
Deported, transferred to Muslim household 1915, reclaimed 1919

[Aunt] Elizabeth Haroian, b. 1912
Deported and disappeared, 1915

The Thirty-Year Genocide: Turkey's Destruction of Its Christian Minorities: 1894-1924. Benny Morris and Dror Ze'evi. Cambridge: Harvard UP, 2019:

> "The Christians of Turkey suffered three decades of persecution even though there were years of relative "quiet" between each murderous bout. This meant that the Armenians—less so the Greeks and Assyrians—underwent an almost unrelenting torment: an Armenian woman from eastern Anatolia, born in the 1880s, would likely have seen her parents killed in 1895 and her husband and son massacred in 1915. If she survived, she probably would have been raped and murdered in 1919-1924. Certainly she would have been deported in that last genocidal phase." (page 502)

See page 116 for elaboration on Morris and Ze'evi's quote based on the oral histories contained herein.

Contents

AT FOUR O'CLOCK
IN THE AFTERNOON

GULEEG HAROIAN, née TOOMASIAN

Translated by Rose D. Guerin, PhD
Edited by Gil Harootunian, PhD
Afterword by Rebecca Jinks

Region Map

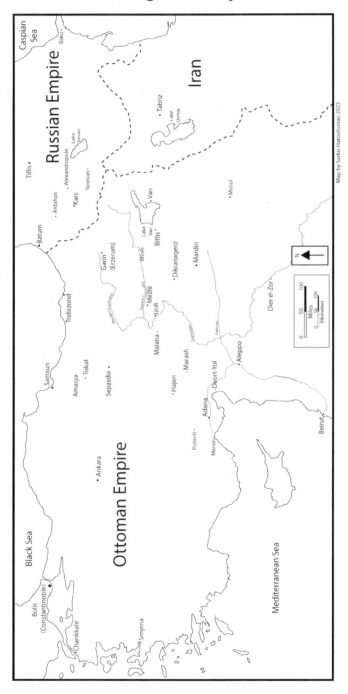

Map by Sarkis Haroutiunian 2023

Editor's Introduction:
"At Four O'clock in the Afternoon"

Overview

Guleeg Haroian was 10 years old when the Sultan Abdul Hamid ordered the Great Massacres of Armenians throughout the Ottoman Empire. The troops along with local gangs attacked Tadem on October 27-29, 1895. They murdered Guleeg's father, and they stole all the family wealth. The attackers also shot, flayed, and set on fire her maternal uncle, Father Aharon, a priest. Guleeg's grandmother was rendered speechless when the Turks and Kurds dragged her son (Father Aharon) out of the house to kill him. Her grandmother was then murdered—thrown down a wheat well (Kaloosdian, 2015, page 23). During the Great Massacre, mass rapes of the female adults took place (Kaloosdian, 2015, pages 25-26). Muslim raiders kidnapped children and dragged them into their own households until the intervention of on-site Western missionaries secured the release of these children. All children saw their world literally set on fire and reduced to ashes: "Of the 300 houses in Tadem about 250, some of which also contained shops, were burned. The only Armenian houses left standing were those that adjoined the homes of the Turks" (Kaloosdian, 2015, page 25). The horror of the Great Massacres (1894-1896) deepens when one realizes that both past and future massacres would amplify the torment of these women. The Reverend James Wilson Pierce, D.D., a missionary in the Ottoman Empire in the 1890s, writes of the reaction of his Armenian neighbors to the Great Massacres (1894-1896):

> A woman in a house near our own went crazy from fear, and did not recover her reason for days. Many of the older people remember the massacre of 1860, and their horror at the possibility of another such experience is pitiable to behold. (Pierce, 1896, 435)[1]

The people of Tadem struggled to recover for years after the Great Massacres. By 1915, some had even begun to flourish. Guleeg Haroian was 30 years old and had her own family when the Young Turks ruling the Ottoman Empire ordered the extermination of the Armenians in 1915. She lost two of her three children as well as many other family members, including her mother, Vartouhi Toomasian, killed savagely. Guleeg Haroian and one of her daughters (Eva) survived through forced transfer into a Muslim household.

A survey of the literature suggests that Guleeg Haroian's oral history is the only one in the English language of women who survived both the 1895 Great Massacres and the 1915 Genocide.[2] Few may exist even in Armenian, for Vahé Tachjian writes, "…the overwhelming majority of self-narration sources at our disposal were written by men" (2019, page 167).

In general, histories of adult females in villages in the interior are the rarest.[3] The reasons are many: little to no literacy, a limited number of interview transcripts that were not widely published (Derderian, 2005, page 3), limited resources to rescue children and females captured in Muslim households, and the inability to self-rescue post-Genocide. A distinct and equally strong reason is the community taboo that precluded females discussing their sexual trauma. A hard truth is that some Armenian men in the U.S. did not retrieve their wives or daughters if they learned of the woman's forced transfer into a Muslim household. Faced with such a harsh fate, many women endured silence. Documentary director Suzanne Khardalian explains that she tried everything to gain the story of the female survivors in her family, but "I met a wall of silence" (*Grandma's Tattoos*, 17:25). Khardalian elaborates, "It was difficult in the family to talk about this. It was so silenced. There was such a silence about this. Everybody was avoiding me. They were literally avoiding me. When I came, they were running away because they didn't want to talk to me" (*Armenian Grandma's Tattoos Director*, 3:20). Khardalian pieces together vital pieces of information to learn the little that she can about her family history. One of those pieces of information is that her grandmother's father was going to be arrested by the Turks, so he fled (*Grandma's Tattoos*, 15:15). Post-Genocide, her great-grandmother with her two daughters located her husband, but when the husband found out what happened, he told her "To go back to her Islamic man, go back, I don't want you" (*Armenian Grandma's Tattoos Director*, 5:40).

Guleeg Haroian's daughter Eva gives a more detailed oral history of her forced transfer and following three years in a Muslim household. Child survivors who underwent forced transfer into a Muslim home were free to discuss it though many did not because re-telling the story would dig up buried emotional trauma. The knowledge gained from reading together the detailed account of a child survivor like Eva and of an adult female survivor like Guleeg makes one keenly aware of the loss to history from the innumerable stories of females and children that went unheard. Khardalian states it eloquently:

> "The story of those who didn't die, the story of the young women who survived and stayed behind has never been told. Men write down history. So it is with genocide. There is no room for the women. They were impure, tainted, and despised. Yet they were the ones who suffered most. They were the ones who paid a terrible price." (*Grandma's Tattoos*, 33:30)

Guleeg Haroian's History: "...an almost unrelenting torment"

The following two oral histories consist of excerpts from tapes made in 1976 with my grandmother, with myself and my mother, Rose D. Guerin (née Haroian) translator, and in 1987 with my Aunt Eva (Armenian and English speaking). My mother translated the entire oral history of my grandmother. I conducted follow-up interviews with both Guleeg Haroian and Eva Hightaian (née Haroian) for elaboration and clarification. I also consulted my grand-mother's account in a book that the Tadem's Council in America published. I read the book on-site at the Armenian Apostolic Holy Trinity Church on 635 Grove Street, Worcester, Massachusetts.

Guleeg Haroian narrates the destruction of her village … until every Armenian house is empty. That image of emptiness reveals the reasons for Guleeg Haroian operating with decisive autonomy. Guleeg Haroian, née Toomasian, was born in 1885, when patriarchal clans ruled the Armenian villages. Extreme crimes inflicted by the Ottoman Empire destroyed the patriarchal leadership in the Armenian community: in the Great Massacres (1894-1896), Guleeg's father was shot and killed, along with her uncles and other adult males. Guleeg's mother, Vartouhi (Rose), became the de facto head of the household. Despite being in a patriarchal clan society, Guleeg Haroian grew up with an absence of able-bodied men heading the family. One 75-year-old uncle, a male whom Guleeg described as "too old to kill," helped the family to survive. That 75-year-old uncle was able to obtain one wooden plow. He gathered the surviving children, led them to the fields, and had them plant seeds while he plowed. He often stumbled and fell. Guleeg said in anguish decades later, "He looked funny when he fell. We laughed at him. We were children and didn't know." The 75-year-old uncle persisted, the wheat grew, and the women and the children harvested it. They survived.

Guleeg married seven years later, and her husband Hagop Haroian followed the increasingly common path of immigrating to America. Guleeg was head of her own household now. Her daughter Eva shares a story of her father Hagop's sole visit to back to Tadem, before the Genocide, and Eva concludes with this observation of her mother's position as head of the household:

> *"A short while later, he returned to work in America. My grand-mother came to live with us because my mother was young and alone, and beautiful. My grandmother would cook for Mary and I and take care of us, while my mother was head of the house;*

she did the outside chores, she would go work with her friends and cousins in their fields. But she would comb our hair in the morning and send us to school."[4]

In 1915, Guleeg was alone, with three daughters: Elizabeth, age four; Eva, age nine; and Mary, age 11. The Turkish gendarmes first killed the small number of remaining adult males in the village. Only the women stood between their children and death; only the women stood between themselves and their own death. Scholars have noted the 1915 Genocide brought about an "unexpected role reversal" as women became the guardians of their families (Sanasarian, 1989, page 452).

I would note that for some women, that role reversal began with the Great Massacres in the 1890s—and even earlier for some women whose villages and towns underwent earlier massacres or whose clans possessed the wealth, bravery, or beauty that made them targets of the local Turkish and Kurdish *aghas*. The numbers of women experiencing that role reversal increased during the next two decades through the widespread emigration of Armenian men to America or Russia.[5] No life can prepare a person for a genocide, but to the extent any life could, the girls who survived the Great Massacres had begun that excruciating process. They had experience with real-time decision-making under extreme conditions. In 1915, Guleeg Haroian had to make decisions under these conditions:

> "When I was standing with the neighbors, Anna, my brother-in-law's wife, came running. She said, 'Now the village aghas are going to get a policeman, and they're going to take you to the konagh.' That was the Turk's house where they tortured and beat us. The gendarmes already had a group of our men in the konagh, and we could hear them screaming."

This passage provides two insights: the immediacy of the horror of the Genocide for women in the villages (versus towns or cities) and the spontaneous resistance networks of women in these villages.

On-site witnesses routinely describe the immediate horror of the Genocide for females in the villages[6]: "In smaller villages, the men were often killed within sight or hearing of their horrified womenfolk, but in larger towns they were marched away to where their murder would not be witnessed, particularly by foreigners" (Rogan, 2015, page 174).[7] Danish missionary, Jacobsen, writes of the fate of men in one village: "The women told me that all their husbands were taken a little way out from the village where they were killed. The soldiers brought their clothes back and washed them at the spring" (201, page 102). From the first days of the genocidal campaign, the axiom of village females was, *"Save yourself."*[8] The immediacy of the horror of village women is in stark contrast to that of women in the towns and cities. In the city of Yozgat, when the deportations began, the women believed their men had safely been deported to Aleppo, and when ordered to leave to join their husbands, "the Armenian women rejoiced and briskly made preparation for the road. Many of them, as though going on a pilgrimage to Jerusalem, even made sweets— *gatas* and *paklavas*—and arranged them in tin boxes to take to their husbands…" The caravan of about 6,400 women, girls, children, and infants was led away, and then encircled by soldiers, and slaughtered by a mob of 10,000-12,000 local Muslims, who butchered them with "axes, hatchets, scythes, sickles, clubs, hoes, pickaxes, shovels" (Balakian, Grigoris, 2009, pages 141-145; *see also* Akçam, 2018, page 211; Morris and She'evi, 2019, pages 503-504).[9] [10]

Secondly, the passage also identifies another village woman: *"Anna, my brother-in-law's wife,…"* who risked her life by warning Guleeg she was going to be brought in and tortured.[11] This is Anna Haroian (née Sahagian). She was in high danger from warning Guleeg because Anna was sheltering with Khanum Kilivchan, the second wife of Hadji Bego, the Kurdish *agha* who had perpetrated the 1895 Great Massacre in Tadem. One of Hadji Bego's sons, Hafiz, and one of his grandsons, Ashreff, were the village *agha*s who "sated their bloodlust" in the 1915 Genocide (Kaloosdian, 2015, page 133).[12] Anna was sheltering in the same house as the *agha*s who were torturing and murdering the villagers, and doing so on far lesser pretext than a warning to a sister-in-law. Anna must heard the *aghas* talking about going after Guleeg, and her flight to warn Guleeg must have been swift and covert.[13] Guleeg Haroian survived more than once during the worst time of the Genocide through the help of Armenian females like Anna whom Muslim households had captured (as wives, concubines, or servants). During the worst times of collections and deportations, Guleeg's niece Yeva and another villager named Guleeg Karagulian shelter her and her three children.

We also learn that Guleeg Karagulian was never retrieved by her husband in the U.S. because he found out she had escaped the tortures, rapes, and murders of the Genocide by marrying a Turk. Eva Haroian Hightaian confirmed that her own father never knew her mother had married a Turk: no one talked about it while Guleeg Haroian was still alive. At another point, Guleeg Haroian shelters with her niece, Yeva, who is living with a Turkish man, and Eva notes that Yeva had to hide her story, too.[14] Finally, amidst five years of hell-on-earth (1915-1920), Guleeg recalls this one woman (whom she does not name):

> *"We started the journey. There was an Armenian woman from Aleppo with us. We had paid for her because she had sent word to her husband, who had not answered, but she had already taken out her passport.*
>
> *Eva said, 'Mother, our money is a lot. Let's give her some, so she can buy her ticket.'"*

In short, many Armenian women hid sexual trauma and forced transfer into Muslim households so their relatives in the U.S. or Russia would rescue them and/or they would be able to re-join into the Armenian community. In a not atypical example, one survivor giving an oral history requested the tape recorder be turned off when she came to revealing her forced marriage to a Turk (Derderian, 2005, page 11), a standard request:

> *"While gender violence is typically mentioned in accounts of the Genocide as a way to emphasize the suffering of the victims, documentary evidence remains understandably scarce, survivor*

interviews scarcer still. Contemporary observers often cited their discomfort openly discussing sexual violence, and some accounts explicitly expunge passages recounting it, or else summarize it only superficially" (*ibid,* page 6).

Scholars confirm the treatment of these women was "less than magnanimous," with many who had been raped and/or gave birth to illegitimate children being "shunned" even by other refugees (Tachjian, 2009, pages 64-66). Kaloosdian describes the response of Armenian males from Tadem in the United States:

"Family honor became a source of anguish for the handful of Armenian men who learned that their wives had miraculously survived. For some women there would be no return. Their new re-formed families would not retrieve them.

"It was ultimately Bedros Bogohian, Tadem's eloquent chronicler, who witnessed so much of what transpired in the village by being left behind, who spoke up for the dignity of the ravished women.

[Bogohian stated on the Armenian men asking him what are their wives 'doing' back in the old country] "These Tademtsis are out of their minds. 'Why are you asking me that question?' I said. 'What kind of question is that? Don't ask me how they live, ask me if they live. Your women have been tortured like Christ. Bring your wives here, take care of them, respect them" (*2015, pages 260-261).*

Ekmekcioglu writes: "Refugee women either did not write their memoirs or when they did, they did not tackle the issue of unwanted motherhood and babies" (Ekmekcioglu, 2016, page 41). Peroomian comments on the overall lack of scholarship on women, "And here, we come late. Most of these women are dead and buried now, and buried with them are their stories that never had a chance to reach receptive ears and fill a small gap in the history of the Armenian Genocide" (2009, page 14).

The significance of the oral history of Guleeg Haroian is increased because of a highly unusual circumstance for the remote villages. Three parallel narratives exist that enhance Guleeg's narrative: (1) the oral history of her daughter, Eva Hightaian (née Haroian); (2) the *Memoirs of a Soldier About the Days of Tragedy* by Bedros Haroian, her brother-in-law; and (3) Robert Aram Kaloosdian's *Tadem: My Father's Village: Extinguished during the 1915 Armenian Genocide*. These parallel histories provide a more complete picture. For example, when Bedros Haroian escapes from his labor battalion in the Ottoman Army, he arrives at the house of Moustafa *agha* in Mezre to find Bado Haroian and Guleeg Haroian sheltering there. He notes that Bado has lost her oldest son and Guleeg had lost her three daughters in the collections and deportations.[15] The timing is late fall. In her oral history, Eva states clearly that her mother married a Turk for protection during the worst times of collections—during the summer months—when Eva was still hiding in the village with her mother. Eva adds that her mother's Turkish husband took sick and died within three weeks. The conclusion is that Guleeg Haroian brokered two marriages with Muslim husbands. The first husband, an Ottoman soldier stationed in Tadem during the summer when the collections were on going, died suddenly. The second husband, Moustafa *agha*, lived in Mezre, and Guleeg entered his protection sometime in the fall when she was alone and the collections had lessened (simply because most Armenians had been deported).

Examples exist in the literature of the active brokering of marriages by Armenian women. Ekmekcioglu states, "Some women took the initiative and found a Muslim man to whom they would provide sexual services in return for protection from deportation, or to save their immediate kin" (Ekmekcioglu, 2013, page 5128). [16] [17] In *Some of Us Survived*, Kerop Bedoukian notes instances of his mother or other women brokering marriages. His mother helps a distant relative Loosentag survive through marriage to a Muslim and, post-Genocide when the situation of the Armenians was still bleak, his mother counsels Loosentag to remain in the marriage. Bedoukian notes that Loosentag's "marriage" consisted of the young man moving to their house (1978, pages 92-83; 136). He also describes the skill of an Armenian mother who, post-Genocide, sets a trap for an Armenian American by using her 18-year-old daughter as bait but maneuvering him into marrying instead her 22-year-old daughter who had a child "whose father was known to be a Turk" (1978, page 201).

When reading of women actively brokering marriages during and post-Genocide, one has to ask, who else could have? The Genocide targeted and destroyed the Armenian community's patriarchal leadership. The severely limited number of adult Armenian females who had survived constituted the main source of authority left. Similar to Bedoukian's mother brokering the "marriage" of Loosentag, Eva Hightaian mentions that her mother "married" a couple post-Genocide. These women were leveraging every ounce of matriarchal authority they had left to save survivors and maintain the community's social structure.[18] The effort of these women was as immense as the challenge. Tachjian clarifies a survivor's use of the term "bestialization" signifies "the collapse of a whole social structure, under whose ruins ordinary human relations have disappeared" (page 141, 2019). When Bedoukian's family reached their first destination point after the Death March, after many deportees are gone and those surviving were sick, hungry, and passing out, his mother issued this command: "Whoever can stand on her feet will be in charge" (1978, page 56). Bjornlund has noted that the Armenian genocide consisted of a two-staged "gendercide" (2009, page 17). First, the perpetrators killed the men, and then the perpetrators raped, deported, and killed the women and children along the Death Marches or at the concentration camps. A limited number of traumatized adult Armenian females who had endured had to pull those left alive from the rubble. Once again, Khardalian states it eloquently: "They had to carry the heaviest burden of all. They had to regenerate life" (*Grandma's Tattoos,* 33:30).

A final compelling example of an Armenian female is that of Santukhd Bogharian. We do not have Santukhd's own narrative, and so learn of her story only through her son's writing. Tachjian clarifies that he focused on Santukhd's story because of the rarity of any material on woman. He continues, "As this section will show, Santukhd, thanks to her flexibility in a period when her husband was absent, scored a number of decisive successes that helped ensure her family's survival" (2019, 167). Santukhd's most important action is selling or gifting her high quality embroideries, especially to the wife of the Effendi handling the Sultan's properties in their locale, and so securing for her son a job. That job transforms the fortunes not only of the Bogharian family but also of other deportees (2019, pages 167-172). Tachjian concludes by noting that Santukhd was "relatively free to act as she saw fit" and she was able to do so "unconstrained ... by masculine prejudices" (page 171). In sum, the thorough destruction of patriarchal leadership in the Armenian communities not only changed how women act but also changed the community in which they were acting: the women make decisions and take actions in a community where the on-the-ground leadership is matriarchal.

In her follow-up interview, Eva Haroian Hightaian shared that my grandmother had endured two gang rapes as well as married a Turkish soldier to save herself and her children (Hightaian, Personal Interview). While I had clarity on two forced marriages to Muslim husbands, gaining clarity on the two gang rapes was a harder issue to tackle as the editor.

Details in the two oral histories and the follow-up interviews, taken together, point to where and when the first gang rape occurred. Eva stated that it was "so bad" after one gang rape that her mother smashed all the glass in the house (Hightaian, Personal Interview). I returned to my grandmother's oral history, and found an event lining up with Eva's description:

"Hadji Agha *came and started collecting our neighbor's things. He even began taking off the Boghosian's windows and carting them away! I ran out, took a stone, and smashed the windows!*

Hadji Agha *shouted,* "What are you doing, Toomas?"

I said, "I've lost my mind." (I had to say something.) "I've lost my mind. What's going to happen to us?"

He said, "Go hide…. You'd better go hide. The dogs are looking for you. Our konagh*'s dogs who rounded up looked for you and found you were gone. Go hide! I don't want them to find you and shoot you."*

Well, where am I going to go? I have no house, no place. No Armenians. No one…. My Anna! She hadn't been taken.

But then Hadji Agha *started taking off our doors. From America, raincoats had been bought. He searched the house and found them. He saw a coffee grinder, by hand, and snatched that. He said, "You told me there's nothing here."*

"Those things are nothing to my eyes," I said. "Look and find them."

He took rubber boots and antiques. He hauled everything we had away, but I smashed the windows in my house, too! One window, he took.

This window-smashing act follows immediately the first time Guleeg Haroian was collected for deportation—the "sofkeeat" that Hadji Agha mentions. The village *aghas* had locked the women out of their homes at four o'clock in the afternoon and driven them to a collection point (the village square) where the women and children spent the night exposed and terrified. Guleeg Haroian does not leave out the mass rapes and mass sales of women that began taking place the next morning:

"And soon the crier yelled for us to go. I jumped. I knew that place so well! I ran. They had begun separating the pretty ones, the brides, for rape, marriage, and property. They were raping and beating them, then driving them out…. I escaped. I had a stick in my hand. I was in my thirties; my eyes and face I had rubbed all black mud on, so the Turks wouldn't recognize me, and they wouldn't see how young I was….[19] From roof to roof, I jumped."[20]

The probability is *zero* that the Turkish and Kurdish perpetrators who had spent weeks torturing and killing the men and then torturing and raping women in their *konagh,* and who in the morning were selling females for "rape, marriage, and property," did not rape the exposed females that first night in the collection. Danish scholar Matthias Bjornlund (2009) wrote the most compelling, detailed, and insightful study of the systematic and government-sponsored "massive" rapes of Armenian women and girls that became the "norm" during the Genocide (pages 25, 33, 41). Witnesses described the public rapes and sale of women and girls as "a carnival of murder and rape," "orgy," and "bacchanal of barbarity" (page 24). The sexual brutality took place "openly in the streets" (pages 16, 25) and continued over "weeks, sometimes months" (page 24). During the Death March, the 'guards' allowed men from villages they passed through to abuse the females, sometimes even distributing females for the night (page 25). Concentration camps reached by a remnant of ravaged females were "well-organized" slave markets (page 23), which proved to be "a lucrative business for Bedouin and Kurdish tribes" (page 32). One Danish missionary notes, "out of the thousands of Armenian females she had come into contact with, all but one had been sexually abused" (page 24). Bjornlund clarifies that many motivations lay behind the massive and public rapes:

> "...sadism, gratification by total domination, symbolic purification (the exorcizing of 'evil' through rituals of degradation), mutual demonstrations of masculinity in the cases of gang rape, and humiliation, intimidation and dehumanization of the immediate victim," "sport" to break the monotony of weeks of routine killing and rape, and, finally, the government incentivizing "popular male participation in the extermination process." (pages 29-30)

Corroboration of a second and public rape comes from Guleeg Haroian's own oral history. She recounts an assault where two assaulters stripped naked and 'beat' herself and another woman: this is doubtless a rape scene. It is important to remember that rape was—literally—unspeakable: the word "rape" was not in the common vocabulary at that time and in that place. An extensive review of the literature on the Genocide indicates the word "rape" was also not common in the language of foreign missionaries and officials. Only Maria Jacobsen, a Danish missionary, uses the word "rape" clearly and consistently. The range of substitute words or phrases for rape—e.g., a female was abused, maltreated, violated, outraged, the soldiers inflicted their criminal will upon the girls, and so on—makes for a lengthy list (*see* Haroian, Bedros, 2021, page 382).

As Guleeg narrates the savage assault, she includes this detail: the "wife of a Turk" who had accompanied Guleeg and her friend remained untouched during the savage assault. Guleeg Haroian noting the safety of the "wife of a Turk" during the second rape suggests this moment was determinative in her decision to seek that protection:

> *The Turks are still looking for me! What to do? I decided to go to Mezre[21] and see if my in-laws were there so I might make a place for us. I left with two other women I knew. The government soldiers got news and came after us on the road to take two of us. The other Armenian woman had married a Turk, who had sent a guard with us: "Take her for safety." But the guard was evil. He said, "I'm afraid" and left us alone. The soldiers came and took the wife of the Turk aside, where she sat down. They had betrayed me, that I still had money.*

> *Then did the gendarmes beat us two!*

> *They took me, and they beat me. In my hair, I had tied ten pieces of gold because in our country, we covered our heads with shawls. The gendarmes stole my shoes, then took my clothes and made me naked. They robbed my money. They kept beating me and beating me. They shouted, "To the sofkeeat![22] There were trees at the side of the road. I grabbed one and held on. They beat me with the rifle butts, but I wouldn't let go of the tree. They put their knives to our throats.*

> *I cried out, "They're going to slay us."*

Then I looked and saw a horseman coming. He was a near village's imam, the Kurd's holy man. He saw the dogs, and he was angry. He yelled, "You can kill the Armenians, but you can't strip the women naked and beat them!" He took us away.

A disquieting thought is that Eva revealed only one marriage (the first marriage to the Turkish soldier who died unexpectedly) because that was the only marriage of which Eva had immediate knowledge. Eva revealed two gang rapes, but that does not rule out more rapes. The sexual violence against Armenian women began well before the first collection and persisted well after, particularly in villages. Many scholars have noted the immediate slaughter of the males made "sexual violence against women in remote locations easier" (see for example Sanasarian, 1989, page 453). One Danish missionary, Jacobsen, writes of Tadem and the rapes of women:

"1 June. From Tadem news is coming that 100 zapties went there. Plundering and arrests have begun. The women and girls had to flee to the mountains to escape persecution from the zapties. It is so terrible every-where, these zapties and soldiers coming in the night and going on at them, now that there are no men to defend them" (Jacobsen, 2001, page 65). U.S. Ambassador Morgenthau also writes of this (again, avoiding the word "rape"), "The gendarmes treated women with the same cruelty and indecency as men…." to the point that "Armenian women and girls, on the approach of the gendarmes, would flee to the woods, the hills, or to the mountain caves" (1919, page 305).

Eva Hightaian in her oral history and follow-up interview recounts how during those weeks Guleeg Haroian escaped to the mountains each morning: "My mother, every morning, went with the shepherds to the moun-tains, on her knees, so they wouldn't know there was a person going, so they couldn't get at her. She went in the morning and came in the night with the shepherds, to see us, to stay with us, and then go again the next morning. When the soldiers knocked on the door, they asked for the head of the house, which was my mother. We said, "We don't know. She's not home. We don't know where she is." They came inside and looked all through the house, in all the closets, they looked everywhere, but they could not find her."

When Guleeg Haroian makes the decision to marry a Muslim, she is making the decision that airline staff drill into adult passengers with children: in an emergency, secure your oxygen mask first, and then secure the oxygen masks of your children.[23]

Her choice was a last resort because Young Turk policy did not allow Armenian women to bring their children into the home of their Muslim husband. The children had to be hidden or given over to an Ottoman orphanage or Muslim homes for "upbringing and assimilation" (*terbiye ve temsil*), meaning Islamization (Maksudyan, 2019, page 18). The treatment of Armenian children in the orphanages was so bad that many died. Moreover, to finish up the Genocide, eventually the Armenian orphans were murdered: "some of them were blown up in their carts with dynamite in an utterly uninhabited spot in the desert, while others were put in natural cavities in the ground, sprinkled with kerosene, and burned alive" (Kévorkian, 2011, page 667; Bjornlund, 2009, page 34; Maksudyan, 2018, page 18). In Ourfa, an American missionary wrote of the Armenian children gathered in an 'orphanage': "The one, to me, most terrible thing, was the shutting up of two thousands or more children in several houses and their being left there for several weeks and then the houses opened and the bodies taken out" (Barton, 1998, page 113). Danish missionary Jacobsen writes of the fate of Armenian orphans in Mezre on 22 October 1915: "All the Armenian children who had been collected together in Turkish children's home have been taken away in ox-carts and thrown into the river" (2001, page 99). Turkish scholar Akçam documents the mass killing of Armenian orphans in Aleppo, Meskene, and Rakka (2018, pages 135-150).

Guleeg Haroian was not going to surrender her children to one of the Turkish orphanages. She decides instead to hide her children and succeeds in doing so for months—until the final collection. She goes out to find food, and her children hide in a haystack with a few other Armenians who have managed to evade collection. The Turks sweep the village and fields, plunge their swords into the haystack, and hit one man, who cries out. The Turks destroy the haystack and collect everyone for the *sofkeeat*.

One more factor distinguishes these unique oral histories: each reveals the thought processes and real-time decision-making during the Genocide. First, Guleeg Haroian's narration reveals the cognitive dissonance of an adult experiencing the first mass Genocide in the 20th century:

> *"Because the massacre in 1895 had lasted three days, we kept thinking, 'Now there isn't going to be anymore. Today, they will give us our freedom. Tomorrow, we'll be saved.'"*[24]

With increasing panic, Guleeg begins to realize that something disturbingly worse than a brutal massacre is taking place:

> *"... the soldiers are counting, by numbers, and they wanted me. The Turks had counted them, and they had counted me. They counted everybody."*

The counting—not only the collecting and killing but also the counting—is relentless:

> *"The Turks had counted again.... The soldiers were still collecting wherever there is* **one** *Armenian left. They're taking them out of the village to slay them. Every village, not just ours. In the summer they started, in May. Until the end of November, they killed."*[25]

When Guleeg Haroian eventually makes the decision to escape from the collections, she holds onto four advantages. One advantage was unexpected and a result of wartime: Tadem had many Muslim soldiers stationed there, and not a few wanted wives, especially wives for whom the Muslim soldiers did not have to pay the traditional dowry. Three advantages came from a lifetime in Tadem. Guleeg knew where to find hiding places, she knew where to find water, and she knew a small number of Turks, Kurds, or the Armenian women who had married them, who might help her and her children. To illustrate, when Guleeg takes her three children to a good hiding place in the village, a man is hiding nearby, and when he hears them speaking Armenian, he reveals himself and asks for help.

"He said, 'I'm thirsty.'

There was a brook near, so we brought water. 'Wherever you're hiding, go back there,' I warned.

'What's going on?' he asked.

'Don't ask,' I said. 'Just look to save your life.'"

Post-war, Guleeg Haroian is able to self-rescue, and then to reclaim her daughter. Guleeg Haroian goes on to work for the *vorpahavak* (collection of orphans), reclaiming children as well as young brides captured in Muslim homes.[26] As a *vorber havak'ogh* (orphan collector), one hears Guleeg counting every one of those Armenian orphans she reclaims:

During this wait, I would go to the government and tell them, an Armenian person is in this place, and I'm going to get this boy, that girl. I would bring our survivors to the Red Cross headquarters....

... I saw our Toros. Boghosian. A sack on him and all over his body, sores. He was in a hug position, sitting in the street. He was six or seven years old.

"Toros?" I said.

He looked. "Ahaaeeee."

"Come," I said. "I'm taking you to the American Red Cross." He had no one. The family had all been massacred. The Americans came and examined him, and they separated him, all sores, into a room. When I got up in the morning, he had run away.[27]

.... There was a bride in another city. I went. I took a government official, got her out, and brought her.

.... Melkon I saved from the village.

Tachjian showed interest in the decision-making of these women: "There were those who determined to survive the tragedy, and we think the Armenian women in this category [forced marriages or sexual relationships] formed the majority.... In these circumstances, the methods used to survive ... were often superhuman or simply failed to conform to the normal human values and traditional conduct of a group of society (2009, pages 76-77; see also pages 64-66). I would elaborate that details in the highly limited material available suggest these women were *driven* to survive—for themselves, for their children, and for their nation. For instance, when Guleeg Haroian learns that Eva has survived and is living in Mardin, she risks her life to travel to reclaim her daughter. A wealthy and powerful Arab family has adopted Eva, and she hesitates to leave them. Eva is non-plussed by her mother's rage toward the Arab family that has adopted Eva and is content to keep her. When Eva finally departs with her mother, she is non-plussed that her mother forbids her to speak Arabic and sells all of Eva's Arabic belongings, including precious gold jewelry.

Bedoukian portrays his mother as driven in the same way. When a Turkish boy who is courting his sister tosses over their fence a "delicacy fit for a king" ("six ripened, dried poppy heads, the seeds still in them"), at night his mother and sister take the bundle, dip it into the latrine, and toss is back over the fence into the Turkish boy's yard (1978, pages 93-94). Bedoukian writes, "No matter what the repercussions, we have to show him that we might have lost a lot, but we still had our dignity" (page 94).

Tachjian presents a parallel between these Armenian female survivors and survivors of the Holocaust: "for Jews, survival itself was a constant act of resistance, because the Nazis had targeted them for extinction" (Ofer and Weitzman, cited in Tachjian, 2009, page 76). Ofer and Weitzman point out that this "understanding of the resistance runs counter to the traditional historiography of the holocaust, where there is an inclination to consider only military acts against the Nazis as truly heroic" (cited in Tachjian, 2009, page 76). Khardalian's documentary reminds us that Armenian culture prescribed one heroic role for these women: "If we think for a minute, and remember what they were teaching us at school, it is something that makes me very angry today. They were always telling us, 'And the women decided to jump into the water and take their lives. Yes, some did. The majority did not. Life is very precious…. Of course, these women choose life to death" (*Armenian Grandma's Tattoos Director*, 10:35). This definition equating 'heroism' with self-inflicted death renders women who survived … despicable. Khardalian emphasizes, "These women were the ones who had to regenerate life, and when I say life, I mean Armenian life. These were they women who gave new children so the Armenian nation could continue" (*Armenian Grandma's Tattoos Director*, 11:40).

Tachjian had arrived at the same conclusion: "It is the generations that were born to these survivors that today form the majority of the Armenian diaspora, as well as a significant number of the citizens of the Republic of Armenia" (2009, page 78). Combining Tachjian's insights with those of another scholar as well as the facts in Guleeg Haroian's oral history reveals that full impact of these women on the Armenian nation. Scholar Watenpaugh had arrived at a parallel conclusion on child survivors: "The Armenian community itself is today, to a significant extent, a community of descendants of children who faced their own forced transfer" (2013, page 286). Guleeg Haroian's oral history reveals that she not only survived but she went on to work for the *vorpahavak*, collection of orphans, and rescued child survivors. This opens the understanding that the generations born to the adult women survivors form a good number of Armenians today *and* the generations born to the droves of children these adult women saved form an additional good number of Armenians today. The agency of women like Guleeg Haroian, taken cumulatively, was consequential to the survival and re-construction of the Armenian community. How consequential is revealed by the fact that 100,000 – 200,000 children and women underwent forced transfer during the Genocide, and current estimates are that less than 20,000 were reclaimed post-Genocide (*see for example* Sarafian, 2010, pages 211 and 217).

When news that Eva is alive reached Guleeg, she faces traveling through lawless territory[28] to reach her daughter in Mardin.[29] Guleeg is willing to risk this, but when she approaches others about travel arrangements, they are not willing to risk it:

> He said, "The last time I came, I took six Armenians, and the gendarmes took them from my hands. They tortured them. I don't want to take you. Wherever you are, stay there."

Guleeg Haroian finally finds a head of a supply caravan travelling to Mardin who is willing to take her. In this breathtaking moment, the moment in which she can reclaim her one living child, Guleeg states that she could travel only if she had papers identifying her as the wife of a Turk to secure her safety[30]:

> "The head, a Turkish merchant, said to me, 'I'll take you as my sister as long as you don't go as an Armenian. I'm going to get a paper from a general that this soldier is in Mardin in the hospital, and you are his wife who wants to go to him.' He gave this information from his mouth and my mouth to the Turkish officials.[31] When they gave me the paper, it made me secure. That paper had a lot of respect. So, I am going as the 'Turkish soldier's wife.'"

During the travel, my grandmother is careful that even her under-clothes are Turkish in case of attempted sexual assault:

> "I said to Altoun, 'Don't say a word. If they find out we're Armenian, it is very bad.' We went with them, still as Turks, to Mardin. One of the men had married an Armenian girl, but we gave no recognition of any kind. Even underneath, I'm wrapped like the Turks are, so if they grab my shawl, I'm still a namaran, the Turkish lady no one sees."

Guleeg Haroian is able to travel convincingly as a *namaran* due to the close cultural and linguistic exchanges between Armenians and Muslims, especially in the villages. Tadem was one of many Armenian villages, and its residents spoke Armenian, including the local Turkish or Kurdish *aghas*. Kaloosdian in *Tadem: My Father's Village: Extinguished During the 1915 Armenian Genocide* mentioned that the Turkish governor and the few Turkish families in Tadem spoke Armenian. A child survivor who endured by slaving in the fields with the other handful of surviving Armenian children, says, "We spoke to each other in Armenian, and our Turkish masters spoke to us in Armenian" (page 148). Guleeg Haroian's history reveals where those Turkish and Kurdish men had learned Armenian. She is about to set out on the journey to Mardin, and she is discussing with her fellow traveler Altoun the need to hide their Armenian identity, when a Turkish man interrupts them:

> *"'Sister, I can speak Armenian. You can talk freely. I understand.'*
> *He had married an Armenian wife before."*

When the supply caravan in which Guleeg Haroian is travelling arrives at Dikranogerd, a city on the way to Mardin, the head receives a telegram stating English troops have surrounded Mardin. The merchant decides to turn back. Guleeg and her companion Altoun decide to press on; they choose to travel through the lawless countryside, and to do so alone:

> *"We walked and walked. Our shoes became torn apart. We were*
> *barefoot, bareheaded. The rain began pouring. We got soaked from*
> *head to toe. We slept behind big stones. We walked and walked."*

They succeed in reaching Mardin, where Guleeg Haroian locates her daughter Eva. Guleeg begins to arrange for their departure to America and, during this time, she shows unflinching agency every day, all day, as a *vorber havak'ogh* (orphan collector). Her acts of reclamation of Armenian children and females continue to the final moments of her exodus from Mardin: working with the Armenian doctor at the local hospital, she boards the last train out. Her task is to manage a car full of Armenian brides whose train car the Armenian doctor has arranged to quietly separate from the train car with their Turkish soldier husbands. The brides' car with the brides will end up in Aleppo, and the car with the Turkish husbands will end up in Adana.[32]

Guleeg Haroian's capacity to act decisively saves herself and Eva one final time. She had left her native province of Kharpert to journey to Mardin to retrieve Eva during the narrow window of time between November 1918 and late 1919. In that period, the Kemalist resistance emerged, the situation on the ground was changing rapidly, and the Turkish government openly showed their hostility to forcing its population to relinquish its Armenian captives. Guleeg Haroian's whole life had taught her the insecurity of being an Armenian in the Ottoman Empire, whose true law was Shari'a Law. She trusted neither time nor laws. Her swift and decisive action enabled her to reclaim Eva and herself. Had she not done this, their lives would have been at immediate risk during the 1919-1924 'clean up' job of exterminating the Armenians enacted by the new Kemalist government (Morris and Ze'evi, 2019, page 502). During a time of "...*an almost unrelenting terror*," she acted with agency.

Note: *[Pause]* indicates a moment so disturbing that Guleeg Haroian had to pause and collect herself.

Maps and Place Names

All maps were created by Sarkis Harootunian in 2021 using Adobe Illustrator for Bedros Haroian's *Memoirs of a Soldier about the Days of Tragedy* and updated in 2023 for this book.

Place names used on the maps and throughout the text are Western Armenian transliterations. I tried to place as many mentioned locations on the maps as possible. Place names are primarily the names used at the time of the event. Numerous places are referred to by their Armenian name and their Turkish name in the same section. Those place names are left in both languages. Several small villages mentioned could not be located.

The primary source for Western Armenian spelling of villages and cities is *Armenians in Ottoman Turkey: A Geographic and Demographic Gazetter,* Sarkis Y. Karayan, London, Gomidas Institute, 2018.

Locations displayed on the maps are from base maps and:

- *Armenia: A Historical Atlas,* by Robert Hewsen, Chicago, University of Chicago Press, 2001. Multiple pages;
- "Kharpert and Neighboring Villages." *Tadem: My Father's Village: Extinguished During the 1915 Armenian Genocide.* by Robert Aram Kaloosdian, Portsmouth, NH, Peter E. Randall Publisher, 2015. page 8. Map.

The base maps used in creating the maps:

From the Army Map Service, U.S. Army:

Harput-Elazig 1942 from Turkish original dated 1938;

"Map of Turkey, Armenia, Azerbaijan, and Asiatic territories formerly Turkish, now under the administration of various Allied powers."

> "Map of Turkey, Armenia, Azerbaijan, and Asiatic territories formerly Turkish, now under the administration of various Allied powers." *Commercial Atlas of Foreign Countries*, Chicago, Rand McNally and Company 1921, p. 50. Map.
>
> —*Sarkis Harootunian*

Kharpert Map

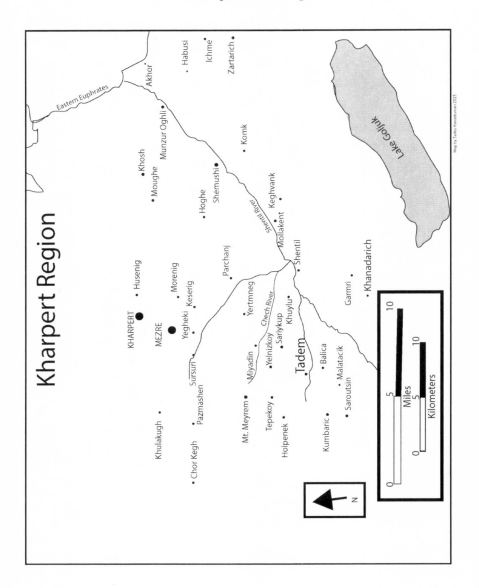

"At Four O'clock in the Afternoon"
by Guleeg Haroian

On the 1894-96 Great Massacres,[35]
Taking Place in Tadem on October 27-29, 1895:

I was ten when the Turks killed my father George in the village. The Turks wanted to steal our wealth. Mamood *agha*[36] arrested my father and demanded, "Give me your money!" After, he shot my father, and our wealth was taken to his house.[37] Then the Turks came and burned our house into a pile.

My mother's brother, a priest who had baptized me, also died here.[38] The killing went on for three days. Some of us had run and hidden in the house of Hadji Memahd. The Turks came to clear us out, and everyone ran this way and that. I felt sick. I jumped under the quilt with my grandmother.

The Turks grabbed my uncle, the priest.[39] When they dragged him out, my grandmother lost her speech.[40] They shot him in the leg and left him to die. Some Armenian men found him and carried him halfway on the road to Mezre, but his wound got cold, and he could not go any further. They made a stone pile, hid him behind it, and went to Mezre to get help. By the time they came back, a Turkish peasant had spied my uncle and gave the news to others. The Turks came, shot him, and burned him.

…children were given to the orphanage,[41] but my mother and another uncle said, "Our children will not go to the orphanage!" My uncle was 75 years old; he went with my mother, myself, his daughter-in-law, and her little sons, Mampreh, five years old, and Samuel, seven years old, into the fields.[42] [43] [44] We ploughed. We sowed. We reaped. We became all right; we hired workers; we rebuilt the house.

We had been very rich before that massacre. We had several large fields, and many, many donkeys, oxen, sheep, and cattle. Even in the winter, there were four laborers. In the summer, we had twenty to thirty workers. They cultivated, sowed, and planted cotton; they threshed the wheat, five hundred bushels of wheat. My family had been altogether twenty heads. We were five sisters and four brothers, and I was the youngest.

Seven years after that I married Hagop Haroian. We had two daughters, first Mary, and then Eva. In a few years, Hagop went to America to work, but in 1911, after the Young Turks' promised freedom, Hagop came back. I had two more children, Elizabeth[45] and then George. He was named after my father. A crazy man in the village used to come knock on our door and say, "God sent me for George." George soon died as a baby,[46] before the *aksor*,[47] the shootings and deportings.

On 1915 Genocide:

In 1913, Hagop went to get his passport. He believed the Turks would make him be a soldier, and he did not want to fight for them because they would give him trouble as an Armenian. In every regiment, they would allow a few Armenians.[48] Hagop would be under the Turkish government's arm. When he was free, he could be brave and protect us, but under the arm of the Turkish government, he could not help anyone. He said, "One day, they are going to destroy us, whether they call us brother or not. I'm going to America so I can get my home and family out of this dog country." He went for his passport; the Turks refused to give it.

When that region's *Effendi*,[49] who knew Hagop, came by later and saw us, he said, "Hagop, what are you talking about with Toomas?[50] You are thoughtful. What's on your mind?"

Hagop answered, "I need to go to America because all my money's gone, but they won't give me a passport."

However, some Turks would bring the Armenians over for money, so the *Effendi* said, "In the morning, get ready and collect your belongings. I will bring you your passport. If you want, I'll bring Toomas' passport, too."

Hagop said, "No, she can't come." I was *tzair-odk* ("heavy-footed," meaning pregnant), so I could not go on the road.

Hagop told me, "I'll go, and then you come."

He left his house; he left his property. He gave gold pieces to the Turks and went. He would send us money from America.[51] Soon, the Turks took the men as soldiers. The roads were closed.[52] No news came from America, and no money.[53]

The Turkish officials[54] brought from the city two or three groups of soldiers, who began destroying and crushing our homes. Nearly all the homes in Tadem were Armenian; we had all been born and raised there. There were only a few Turkish houses, whose Turks had come from somewhere else and settled in Tadem, except for one Turkish family who had been born there.

Of these Turkish soldiers, Hafiz was the first of the scoundrels.[55] He was the biggest murderer of our villagers. He led this first occupation of Tadem. He gathered people in his house and beat them, both men and women. He personally beat Sarkis Nordigian, Kapriel Norsoyan, and Antreas. He took bribes from the women. He beat them countless times and made them stand on their feet for hours. He murdered Kevork Aloyan, the Tiko boys, Garabed Pehlivanian, and many more.

Then soldiers came and surrounded our own house. "Where is your husband's gun?" they demanded. They looked at the walls because the *Effendi* had often seen Papa's sword hanging on the wall.[56]

"Where is the sword?" they said.

"You told him to take it with him."

They searched, turned everything upside down, and destroyed inside the home. They didn't find anything. These government soldiers didn't know who I was, so they just went back and told the *Effendi*, "There's nothing."

"No! There's something."

That *Effendi* came himself. As soon as I saw him, I ran out the back door to the neighbor's house and stayed there. The soldiers wrecked and searched and wrecked some more. They said to my mother and children, "Tell us where!" They found nothing. "Where's Guleeg!"

"She's not here. She went to the water, the brook." They went away.

When I was standing with the neighbors, Anna,[57] my brother-in-law's wife, came running. She said, "Now the village *agha*s are going to get a policeman, and they're going to take you to the *konagh*." The *konagh* was the Turk's[58] big house where they tortured and beat us.[59] The gendarmes already had a group of our men in the *konagh*, and we could hear them screaming.

"Oh, my God," I said. "I'm not staying in this village." Since the soldiers were only looking for me, I said to my mother, "Stay with the children. I am going. I won't let them take me to the *konagh*."

I decided to find out whether this was government law or the evil of the village Turks who, over the years, had done killings. But the Turkish police had surrounded the village; no one could leave. Whoever tried to escape, they'd catch.[60] I had to duck out of the village. Anna and I hurried to the *Vali* in Mezre because the *Vali*'s wagoneer was my in-law.[61]

I went in and said, "The village is in this situation. What's going to happen?"

I thought he might help, as a big government official. Instead, he sent more soldiers to give us more trouble.[62]

[Pause]

I said to Anna, "Let's go to our archbishop." When we came to the archbishop, he just said, "Come Thursday, and we will pray. I'll give you communion."

When he went and protested, the Turks sent two police to grab both him and the Catholic archbishop. The police tied them up and dragged them away, with all the heads of Tadem. By this time, there were few men left in our Tadem village. If there were any, they were hiding or disguised as Turks or Kurds.

I remained out of Tadem, in Mezre, three or four days. Where could I hide in Tadem? The Turks, Kor Zulo and his dog brother, found out and sent police after me and Anna: "We want these two wives." The Turks had done with the men. Now they were gathering the women.

When we got word, I said, "We'll go. Why not? They know where we are." But I whispered to Anna, "I'm not leaving Mezre. I'm going to duck in somewhere. Wherever I go, try to go with me." I wasn't going back. I wasn't going to the *konagh*. I went out and started walking in the right direction. Some man opened a door. I ran in. He just shut it and said, "Don't make a sound." I never knew who the man was.

The two soldiers the Turks sent to look for us on the road captured two women in our place. When they brought in their captives, the *Effendi* said, "These are not the two I want! I want the wives of the Haroian brothers!"[63]

In the meantime, we had fled to Yegheki, where I had a brother-in-law.[64] He told me, "I heard they've taken your mother and children to the *konagh* and are giving them the trouble."

"I have to go."

"No, stay here," he said. "They're going to kill them anyway. If you go, they'll torture and kill you, too."

I could not sleep that night. My children they took to the *konagh!* My nine- and eleven-year-old children in the *konagh!* I could not stay. I woke Anna, and we got up to leave. My sister cried, my uncle cried, "Don't go! Don't go!"

"No! We have to go!"

We left, and on the road we met a captured group of men, all tied together, from our village. The Turkish soldier said to me, "Mother, where are you going?"

"We're going to the village."

The Armenian men cried, "Don't go! We don't wish you to go. When we left, they were burning the village."

My children burned! My mother burned! I saw a familiar neighbor. "Toro! Toro! They say my mother has been taken to the *konagh!* My children!"

"When we were coming, your mother came to the fork and was listening to us. She was holding the children's hands."

They had to go on; the Turks killed them outside Mezre.

I went back to Yegheki. I had no tongue left in me from all this, and I fainted. They took blood from my arm.

I stayed two or three days, until Sahag from our village came and said, "It's been decided. Your family is supposed to leave Tadem on Thursday. Your mother says to come, so you'll go together." The Turks had decided the days for each deportation: Mezre is going this day, that village is going that day.

We got up and walked to Tadem.

Immediately, that village Turk, Ashreff,[65] came and sniffed around, "Poor ones, where is Guleeg? She has to collect her property, so she'll go."

Another Turk I knew replied, "Her husband is in America. She's not going."

"No! She is going so her children and she will be slain, so her husband will die in America!"[66]

The Turks were collecting everyone. At four o'clock, they drove us out.[67] Ashreff sealed all the houses, cursing and leaving Armenian women and children in the street.[68] He took our keys and locked our doors. When they had been collecting the weapons before, this Ashreff had supervised attentively from the fortress. He had our priests Kourken and Antreas beaten. He had gone and sung with the muezzin from the fortress, declaring, "Don't mix with these people! Massacre the infidels!" He himself had the head of Puig Khayo[69] crushed.[70] He had Hovannes der Minassian burned, and then he took part in the destruction of our Church.

Driven from our homes, we slept the first night near the spring.[71] The brook was between two houses; our fountains were outside. The Turks had brought us—*Oh, lord!*—to my father's old fields! Toomasian fields![72] My old house was opposite these hills! It's all the place I know."

Some Turks came that night and said, "Let us take you here. Let us take you there." I wouldn't go. I didn't trust them. I hadn't known a Turk who could be the simple friend of an Armenian. There was one who, expecting some reward from an Armenian, was a friend, but that same Turk would harm another Armenian. So, I remained and spent the night thinking how Ashreff had threatened us.[73]

In the morning, this *fedayee* said, "Get up, each of you, and gather your children."

The *aksor* was going from here. I prepared some chicken and what-not, thinking when we went, if we were hungry, we could eat. I gave these to Hagop's sister[74] to take and said, "I'm going. I can't answer to where I'm going."

The officials had told everyone, "The government is moving the Armenians to another country. They're angry. The Armenians will be poor."[75] They hadn't talked about the slayings and the killings. They were fooling the people. But I wasn't going. When that Hafiz had supervised the first deportation of Tadem and Khoolakiugh, he had ended up throwing crowds of people into the waters of Izol, and he had sold women and girls to the Kurds; he also arranged forced marriages in return for bribes. [76]

I gave the children a little bread,[77] and I gave them several gold pieces. I put my little daughter Elizabeth, four years old, on Eva's shoulders. "Sneak to your aunt's house. Your grandmama is there." They wouldn't go. I got angry: "Go to our house! If I come by night, all right. If not, get up and go to your aunt and grandmother's house." Finally, they snuck away.

Soon the crier yelled for us to go.[78] I jumped. I knew that place so well! I ran. They had begun separating the pretty ones, the brides, for rape, marriage, and property. They were raping and beating them, then driving them out.[79] [80]

I escaped. I had a stick in my hand. I was in my thirties; my eyes and face I had rubbed all black mud on, so the Turks wouldn't recognize me, and they wouldn't see how young I was.

From roof to roof, I jumped.[81] My children were gone, and my stomach was on fire. Am I going to find my children or not? I leaped down two walls so I could reach my children. There were porches sticking out, and I fell. I could hear the Turks on the other side. I kept going.

I found my children sitting near the bee house. "My sweethearts, you're here."

"You came! You came!"

"Yes, I came."

The little one said, "Water, water, water. There's a man."

This Armenian man was hiding and was hungry. He had come and hidden beneath the house.

When he heard our noise, he had come out to see who we were, and he asked us, "My sweets, did you see my children?"

Eva remembered: "Your daughter-in-law and children they separated and took to the *konagh*, but your wife and daughter, no."

He said, "I'm hungry and thirsty. I was a week in the oven."[82]

I gave him the bread and chicken we had left. All the house doors were locked, so I had to find a rope to lower Eva through the roof's smoke-hole to get a lot of bread. Our barrel was full. She gathered some things, and I pulled her up. I decided to tiptoe around and see what was going on in the village.

A Turk named Ahmed was collecting the biggest wealth from the empty Armenians houses,[83] then destroying them; he was taking almost all the doors, too, as well as our stones, holy and carved, from our graveyards and buildings. Nearly all the Turks were looting—Hussein, Moheiddin, Slo, Shukur, Alosman, Usuf,[84] Tomo Hassan from Khokh, and Iman Sheik Abdullah. Some Turks even followed the caravan of the deportation to massacre the Armenians, then grab the money and clothes from out of the blood.[85] They returned to the village full.[86]

Hadji Agha came and started collecting our neighbor's things. He even began taking off the Boghosian's windows and carting them away![87] I ran out, took a stone, and smashed the windows!

Hadji Agha shouted, "What are you doing, Toomas?"

I said, "I've lost my mind." (I had to say something.) "I've lost my mind. What's going to happen to us?"

"Are you alone?" he asked.

"No, my children are here."

"Give me your children to take to the collection, the *sofkeeat*, and I'll free you."[88]

"No. My three children against my life I will never give you. You stand me up and shoot me. I would not trade one life for three."

He cried when I said that, and I started to cry.

He said, "Go hide. I wouldn't shoot anyone. You'd better go hide. The dogs are looking for you. Our *konagh*'s dogs who rounded up the *sofkeeat* looked for you and found you were gone. Go hide! I don't want them to find you and shoot you."

Well, where am I going to go? I have no house, no place. No Armenians. No one.... My Anna! She had not been taken.

But then *Hadji Agha* started taking off our doors. From America, raincoats had been bought. He searched the house and found them. He saw a coffee grinder, by hand, and he snatched that. He said, "You told me there's nothing here."[89]

"Those things are nothing to my eyes," I said. "Look and find them."

He took rubber boots and antiques. He hauled everything we had away, but I smashed the windows in my house, too! One window, he took.

He said, "Oh, Toomas, oh, Toomas, I can't help you," and left.

Nighttime finally came. I said to Eva, "Go and see if your Anna *booboog* is in the house. Have they saved *khanum*?"

She went and came. "Mama, Anna said, 'Let her come to this home. There's a lot of Armenians hiding there.'"

I took the children and crept to this woman's house, where I left them so they could sleep. The gendarmes were still looking for me, so I hid in the connected house. I told my children, "If they ask, cry and scream and say your mother's gone to the *aksor*. If anyone says, 'Come, we'll take you here or there,' do not go."

When I went to hide, didn't that *Effendi* who hated me spy me! This house is that Turk's, and right across is the house we're hiding in. He had been walking on the roof and saw me.

"I'm going to kill her," he said. "She escaped again. How did she escape?"

But his father didn't let him. His father came and nailed all the doors shut in the house to lock us in. He boarded it, so when we hid the Turks wouldn't look there and shoot us.

I didn't come out. The Turkish gendarmes were searching and searching for me. They smelled me around there, and they started looking. The owner of the house, who had hidden inside, said, "My girl, you have come here, and now there'll be a bloodbath. They'll find me."

"No!" I said.

But soon they are crashing the door in. There was an ax, and I grabbed it from the wall. The walls were not new wood; they were clay bricks. I smashed one brick, then two, three. I crept onto the other side, into the *marak*, where they store dry hay. Let them come and look!

As soon as I crawled in the *marak*, ooooh, I saw two men hiding in the pile of straw.

"Oooooh," I said. "It's me."

"Oh, it's you," one said. "Don't be afraid."

They were two I had hidden for a month when they escaped from sol-diering. They said, "They bring us food. They've kept us." A Turk kept them.

Because the massacre in 1895 had lasted three days, we kept thinking, "Now there isn't going to be anymore. Today, they will give us our freedom.[90] Tomorrow, we'll be saved."[91]

As I lay there, I could not hear the children's voices anymore. I said, "I'm going out. What if they took my children?"

Tateos said, "When the Armenian women come with the bread, we'll ask."

When one came, I crept to them. "We won't tell on you," they said.

I thought, "If they whisper, others might hear it." But I said, "Who's there? Who isn't?"

"There's a lot of Armenians still hiding in the house. The children are there."

I crept and listened. I heard Eva's voice. Of all of them, she governed. "My mother is in the *sofkeeat*!"

"Where is she?" they demanded. "Go to your mother!"

Eva started crying, "She's not here! No, we won't go! Anna's mother is taking care of us!"

The gendarme said, "What do you eat if you're left here in this house?"

She shouted and cried, "Nothing. We just go in the village and gather some bread or anything from the empty Armenian homes and bring it back and eat it."

The gendarmes finally left.

"Boys, I'm going down," I said. "My poor children. They are crying. What if they give up and go somewhere?"

I crept down that night and took crying Elizabeth to the crumbled Armenian houses, so they won't hear her. There's no one in the empty houses. I stayed with her. In the morning, I ducked back to the same place to check

39

my other two. Anna's mother had hidden them. The Kaloosdian's boy was there, too. He and Eva would go and catch chickens; that is how Armenians hid and ate.

About that time, a nearby Kurd who had been a friend of Hagop's was sent to the village as a guard. As soon as he saw Eva going to the brook one morning, he recognized her and asked, "Where is your Mama?"

"They took her in the *sofkeeat*!" Eva cried and shouted.

"Tell me the truth. Wherever she is, tell me."

"They took her in the *sofkeeat!*"

"Which one?"

"I don't know! The first one!"

"Tell her it's Mamood Chavoosh."

She came and said, "Mama, there's someone looking for you." When she gave me his name, I went to the brook.

He said, "I'm the Catholic church's guard. The government has filled it with supplies. Come over there. Stay there. I can save you in my storage place."

I got up, took the children, and went. My mother came, too. We began sleeping in the church—now the supply depot.

The Turks were guarding everything. There was nothing, nothing. My children and my mother are hungry and thirsty. I snuck out and saw a cow galloping toward its barn. I ran and grabbed it.

Shouldn't that *Effendi* who hated me see me! He shouted, "Guleeg, where are you taking that cow!"

I yanked and ran with the cow.

Later, I said to the Kurd, "This is what happened."

"Don't be afraid," he said.

I killed the cow and made *kavoormah*[92] for us.

In the meantime, that *Effendi* came to the Kurd and said, "This is the place you've got to send her." It was the house where the sick and ailing Armenians had been put together … so the Turks can take and throw them in a pit. Some Armenians who didn't know this had been giving money so they would be separated from the deportations as being ill. The Turks took bribes and told them they were saved, but after the Turks had all their money, they threw everyone into the pit.

The Kurd said to him, "I won't send her. How many Armenians have you got? You work a ploughman, a picker, a milker. Well, Guleeg's going to cook my meals. I'm not giving her up. When you give up yours, then I'll give up mine."

He told us this. I never did make his meals. His family made the food themselves.

Yet, since an Armenian girl had married a friend of his and lived around there, we decided to go to there. We do not take chances.

Then the Turks began gathering any remaining Armenians. I got up and ran to the house of my aunt's son. Two or three years before, he had become a Muslim. I entered to see he had taken in a mother and daughter with him. Those two Armenians did not want me because the soldiers are counting, by numbers, and they wanted me. The Turks had counted them, and they had counted me. They counted everybody.

There was a house in back, where my aunt's son took me before the light of morning. Outside, the Turks were still shooting and deporting. They were looking and looking. By night, I escaped, escaped, escaped.

I fled to another house. An Armenian girl was there with her husband, a Turkish soldier, who was lying down very sick. Those people! How much they stole from me so I could hide! My sister had given me a watch and plenty of money. They took everything![93]

[Pause]

When the husband got too sick, the family took him to Mezre, and *Hadji Agha* came to take their things away.

"Dear," he said to me, "the dogs are still after you. They are searching, searching. Come to my house."

"If you'll take my children, too, I'll come."

But he only wanted to keep me. I didn't go. If I had, my children might have gone from there.

My mother came to the house. We slept two or three days. Eva followed my mother there. A Turk who had known Hagop found us and said, "If you get killed, I'll get Eva to Hagop."

The Turks are still looking for me! What to do? I decided to go to Mezre and see if my in-laws were there so I might make a place for us.[94] I left with two other women I knew. The government soldiers got news and came after us on the road to take two of us. The other Armenian woman had married a Turk, who had sent a guard with us: "Take her for safety." But the guard was evil. He said, "I'm afraid" and left us alone. The soldiers came and took the wife of the Turk aside, where she sat down. They had betrayed me, that I still had money.

Then did the gendarmes beat us two!

They took me, and they beat me. I had tied ten pieces of gold in my hair because in our country, we covered our heads with shawls. The gendarmes stole my shoes, then took my clothes and made me naked. They robbed my money. They kept beating me and beating me. They shouted, "To the *sofkeeat*! There were trees at the side of the road. I grabbed one and held on. They beat me with the rifle butts, but I wouldn't let go of the tree. They put their knives to our throats.

I said, "They're going to slay us." Then I looked and saw a horseman coming. He was a near village's *imam*, the Kurd's holy man. He saw the dogs, and he was angry. He yelled, "You can kill the Armenians, but you can't strip the women naked and beat them!" He took us away.[95]

He said, "Dear, who would come out at this time?"

I said, "*Effendi*, the truth is I wanted to go to Mezre to see what's going to happen to us. We have nowhere to stay."

He replied, "Dear, dear, you're not one so I can take you and hide you!" He brought us way near Tadem. He was a good man.

We went into the empty houses where my family was hiding. I said, "Mama, this kind of thing happened to us."[96]

She cried and said, "Why did you come back? You should have stayed there!"

"I came for you. I came so I'd get my children and family, and then go there."

I heard a noise. When I looked, I saw two stones on the bed quilt. I got up and said, "Who is that? Who is that?"

A man whispered, "It's me. It's me. I'm starving to death." He was the owner of the house, and he had dug the ground outside his home and hidden. The Turks had come and chased his woman and children to the *sofkeeat*. When he heard us speaking Armenian, he threw the stones.

I had a little food with me. There was nothing in the house, no yeast cakes, nothing.

I had just gathered a little flour here and there and baked it. Well, I gave that to him.

He said, "I'm thirsty."

There was a brook near, so we brought water. "Wherever you're hiding, go back there," I warned.

"What's going on?" he asked.

"Don't ask," I said. "Just look to save your life."

That place we stayed until a person who knew my mother found us. Her husband had gone into the soldiering. This Armenian girl was so pretty, and her father was a big name. He had lived elsewhere, but he had come to his daughter's house. When he saw my mother one day, he said, 'Vartouhi *khanum*, where have you been? What has happened to you?

She said, "This and that has happened, Mustafa."[97]

He replied, "Gather yourselves and come stay at my daughter's house. I'll be your protector."

We gathered ourselves and went. Melkon's mother (Yeva) came to us from wherever she escaped on the road, with little Melkon on her shoulder.[98] Then her sister came, too. We all stayed there, and we worked for the *khanum*. I milked for her, I went to the fields, I baked bread—anything to save my children, to feed my children.

When I looked, the Turks again surrounded the village. There's shooting! There's deporting!

Khanum came running, "Guleeg! Guleeg! Guleeg!"

"What is it?"

"Quickly! Get your family and come to our side!"

We ran. When we reached there, we saw the other Armenians coming, too.

"Amen, Guleeg," the woman said.

We hid.

Three times the Turks gathered and took whomever they could find left, but I remained hiding in those meadows. After a while, when more and more gendarmes came to drive us out, I got up and fled.

My sister was still alive around there, but they had taken her. The Turks made her, like they made many women with no children, bring flour for the government.[99] The women would starve because there were no men; they did all the work. The Turks made the Armenian women do it. There was only one man there. My sister was carting their flour because she had secured some oxen.[100]

When she saw me, she said, "The Armenian houses are all empty. Amen."

I said, "Sister, that's on my mind."

We hid.

My mother had gone to my other sister's house. She came to me and said, "The Turks gave me orders. I came to see you one more time."

The soldiers were coming once more to take anyone; again and again, they came. The police found my mother and chased her; they chased children, everybody, into the meadow and out of the village. There they slay them. They cut their heads off. A few—half dead half alive—crawled back the next day. They came to the house, and I would put the cut necks together and bandage that for them.[101]

That time, one of my sisters, whose husband had been rich, saved herself by giving money to an *agha* and his wife to hide her in a trunk. I had no money left to give.

And the Turks began collecting, again. My sister gave me five pieces of gold and said, "If they save you, they do. If they don't, they don't. Let the money go." I went to that same *khanum*. She would keep a few different Armenians at a time. She took the gold and said, "I will save you."

They sent me working in the fields. I had the children stay in the house, so they would be safe. If they come out, and I run and hide, they can't; they're so little.

That *Effendi* who hated me came and stood with his rifle before her house twice: "I'm going to shoot whoever is there!"

"There is not an Armenian in my house!" she had shouted. "I have no workers!"

"Give them from your house!" he demanded.

In the middle of the night, the *khanum* woke us up. "Get up. Get up. They're coming. They're taking Armenians. Go hide. I'll tell them your children are mine."

The soldiers were still collecting wherever there is **one** Armenian left. They're taking them out of the village to slay them. Every village, not just ours. In the summer they started, in May! Until the end of November, they killed.

Now there is Yeva, Melkon's mother, with Melkon, and my three children. Mary the *khanum* sent out to feed the lambs. Eva and Elizabeth she let play with her Turkish children.

Meanwhile, I said, "Yeva, let's not tell anyone where we're going to hide. We should go hide by ourselves."

We went and crept in the outhouse, in all that stink. We didn't make a sound.

We made a place and squeezed on the side near the walls. Against the door were the wagon's wheels, heavy, so we should not open it or get out.

All of a sudden, I heard Eva calling, "Mother, mother, we're going! We're going! They're taking us to the *sofkeeat*!"

The *khanum* is giving them!

I struggled and struggled. Eva's yelling. The door didn't open. My strength all left me. "Yeva, help! I have no more strength. I've got to get out! Let them kill us!"

Then Mary came and was crying! She had come back and seen her sisters gone. She started crying.

The *khanum* had said, "Mary, don't cry. I'll keep you."

"No," Mary said. "I want my mother and sisters. Wherever they are, tell me. I'll go over there." She added, "I hear a pounding."

They came "Open the door!" I cried. We had struggled two hours! We went to the house. I couldn't even talk. Eva and Elizabeth gone!

The *khanum* said, "Where were you?"

"Where would I be? You told us to hide to push out my children."

I was all that stink. I washed and put on new clothes. The *khanum*'s brother came and saw me. "Where are you going?" he said.

The *khanum* answered, "The children were given, so she's leaving." They took Eva and the others to Mezre. Eva saw a young official and went up to him.[102] She started crying. The man had pity on her and little Elizabeth. "Where is your mother?" he said.

"She was left behind."

"Why did they take you?"

"They just grabbed us."

"If you go back, could your mother take care of you?"

"Yes."

He gave them a quarter and a little change. He told Eva to take the little one and go. Eva shouldered her and walked to the place where she knew my sister, the one carting flour for the Turks, would pass by. When my sister came, Eva ran to her. She put them on her horse and rode to Yegheki.[103]

The Turks had counted again and found they weren't there. An old Turk from Tadem came and told us the children had been separated. But the others wouldn't let me go out. The Turks were finding all the last, scattered Armenians and killing them. 15 days later, I could finally go. I went and got the children and brought them back.

I said, "There's nothing, there's nothing. No matter what, I'm not staying in this village." The *khanum* told me not to leave, she would save me; she said, "If you have ten children, I will save you." But I was so sick and tired by then. There was to be nothing more, they said, nothing more. I just wanted to get away to a place I did not know. A strange place.

I went back to Yegheki and took an empty Armenian house. There are no owners, no owners. You can sit where you want to sit. Empty, all the Armenian houses are empty.

There were Kurdish and Turkish refugees from the Russian side all over. The Turks' ruler had said, "Get out of Russia, Erzinga, Ezerum. All of you get out, and I'll give you homes here, and I'll give you food. Don't stay there."

The Turks gave them the empty Armenian homes. The refugees were starving, too; they filled the village. One of those women told me, "The Russians didn't say anything to us, but we came." She added, "Ah, pretty bride, where are you going? Marry a Turk. You know there's killing! They're coming to take you again."

My sister had come with me to Yegheki. "Takouhi," I said, "she told me they're going to eat us again."

"*Vak!* Let them digest what they eat or do not eat, the stinkers. They saw you were pretty, so they said that."

We had come to that village bare; we had nothing to bring. The children were hungry. No money, no food. No food, no money. My children wanted, wanted. Does a child know fear? I said, "Sister, stay with the children." I walked and searched, all the villages, near and far, far and near.

The officials kept saying there was peace now for us. Nothing more, nothing more.[104] I decided to go to Mezre. I wanted to find food and return quickly. I got an animal and loaded it with wood to try and sell. Harotiun Altounian, the father-in-law of my brother-in-law,[105] came upon me in the road. He said, "Go to so-and-so's house. From America a letter has come from Hagop." He was fooling me so I would go. He knew I had nothing. They were slaying four or five cows at this butcher's house, and Harotiun could give me meat and bones. The butcher was an Armenian who had turned Muslim in the first massacre. He was *Tademtzi*,[106] too.

As soon as I sat down, we heard a rap on the door. They stuck me in the outhouse because the butcher thought the knock might be collectors.

The gendarme said, "Come, come. In the city they opened a safe house and wrote you down as a witness."

The butcher said, "Your eyes should be blinded! If they opened a house in the city, how do we see it? Your tongue should be sliced! Why don't you say there is a collection? You're going to fake us out and eat us."

When the policeman left, he stuck me in the kitchen near the *kavoormah*. He said, "If I don't return by half the night, look after your own head. Know that they have taken me, too."

I said, "Amen! My children! I have to go."

"If they're there, we'll separate them. If they're not, you can't save them and they'll get you, too, on top of it. How can you save your children? You can't. You can't. I'll go and see."

I knew all that, but I wanted to go. He ran out.

The collectors surrounded the house! On the fire, the *kavoormah* was cooking in the big earth oven. I threw water on it and jumped in. They took every Armenian hiding there but me. I sat there and pled with God, "Oh, Father, don't let them collect my children, oh, Father!" The gendarmes finally turned around and left.

Half the night! Midnight! The butcher came.

"My children! My children!" I cried.

"They're gone. They are all gone. They were collected in the Yehgekoo cemetery."[107]

They had taken the children with my sister Marnos and her baby! I shouldn't have gone for the food! Those two days we should have died of starvation! And it was the very last one! The very last collection![108] What can I do? What can I do? Find someone. I'll give money so he'll go and separate my children. Who can we find to separate them? There is no one, no one! They have all been taken. My mind is not on me.

I ran to the baking place; there was one Armenian being worked as a baker.

"Artapar! Artapar!" I called to him. "My children, my children!"

"Be quiet! Keep quiet! They'll come back and take you, too."

My sister Takouhi found me. She had almost lost her speech. "Let's go," she said. "Let's go. It's only you and me left! There is only one answer for us—to hold our hands and throw ourselves in the river. They have taken them all! They're all dead!"

We started out. The baker stood in front of us. "My dears, stay here and have a drink of water."

We drank. We sobbed and screamed. We couldn't throw ourselves in the water.

[Long Pause]

… for six months, I slept inside my sister's dark house.[109] [110] I never saw the light of day. The orphans used to come and knock on the door: "Mother, mother, we're hungry, mother, we're hungry." If there was a piece of bread or anything in the house, I would give it to them. Typhoid came among us. The grave sickness came upon me, but I didn't die. After, I still wouldn't go out. Doctor Mikahil[111] came and said to the women, "It's from her sorrow. Tell her that her children are in this place or that, and she'll get up and walk. Tell her this news so she'll walk in the sweet air, or she'll lose her mind."[112] [113]

They told me these stories, and I rose.

We were all gathered in my sister's house. Her Turks worked us. We were given a bowl of wheat so we would not starve and a little money. At night, when the Turks saw how well I baked the bread, they all wanted me to go with them: "Come, come to our house and bake for us."[114] I did not want to go work for them! I would make believe I was sick and would run away to Mezre. The remaining people would say I wasn't there. The Turks would wait until I got back so I would bake their bread.

"*Kharnasee!* Damn you!" they'd say.

Later search for children and immigration to America.

I searched, and I searched. For three years. I walked in the Turkish villages. Nothing. I went to the city, the American buildings, for word. Nothing. The orphanages. Nothing. I searched them all, I searched them all. Then, I came back.

Some Armenians told me that in Malatia, an orphanage had opened for Armenian children and a lot of *Kharpertzi*[115] were there. I had to find a way to go, to get news. I knew an Armenian girl who was married to a Turkish soldier. "Mary," I had said, "I'm searching for my children. When you go, look for them."

"Come, and we'll take you with us. We'll say you're our cook."

So, I went, but her husband never let her go to an Armenian place herself.

I left them all, my sister, my home,[116] and I went to Malatia, another region. I would go to all the orphanages on the way. Everywhere I looked, I only found one of our village girls. She said, "I won't go back to Kharpert. My sister and brother are in America. When I get free, I hope they will take me from here. When all my family here has been lost, why should I go back and work for the Turks?"

"That's right," I said.

I got word from my sister: There's money from Hagop at the American consul. My sister had gone to get it. Everyone is starving. The Consul[117] said, "Guleeg Haroian has to come and see us, or we won't give it." He said that because many times someone might have sent money to a person and someone else would get it. That's what they do. You can't blame them. What are they going to do? There are no goods. Depression. Depression. They are hungry. Some used to come and take water and food from us because in Malatia there were a lot of things: wheat, flour, grapes.

When I went to sign permission, the Consul's interpreter said, "There's word of one of your daughters. Eva's alive."

I went crazy! I turned cartwheels, cartwheels! I said, "Garabed *Agha*,[118] can you take me?"

He said, "The last time I came, I took six Armenians, and the gendarmes took them from my hands. They tortured them. I don't want to take you. Wherever you are, stay there."

I went back to the house and told that Mary.

She said, "Wait. We will tell the *Effendi*, and he might send you with his aide."

When we asked, he said, "Never mind my aide. I do not trust anyone to God, now. I won't mix her with anyone to go. Maybe, my rank is high, I can take her."

But then his assignment has been transferred to Kharpert, so they took me back to Kharpert.

A woman from Yegheki came to me when I returned, "Did you see your daughter?"

"What are you saying? Where is she?"

"I saw her in Mardin. I was begging. I was hungry."

This woman had come to Eva's house, and Eva had said, "Mary *Bajii*, what are you doing here?"

She had said, "Who are you that you recognize me?"

"I am Takouhi's sister's child, Guleeg's daughter. Come upstairs, but don't tell anyone you know me. I'm going to give you a lot of things."

When she went up, the woman said, "I know this girl" to the mother who had taken Eva from the Death Marches and adopted her.

Eva ran away with that. She was ashamed. She thinks the woman is an enemy. Eva was alone, you know, and scared.

Miriam *Bajii* told me, "It's a wonderful house. The woman is very good to Eva. From head to toe, she is clean, all silver and gold on her. Don't worry at all."

I will go and work for that woman for a year! I said, "My other children?"

"I don't know about the others."

I got up and went to one of the saved Armenians, that baker for the Germans.[119] I said, "Amen. My child is alive. What am I going to do?"

He said, "We know workers who go. We'll have them bring her."

Eva knows these workers, for one is my aunt's daughter-in-law. I told a letter,[120] and she took it. She went and asked, "Is our cousin's daughter here?"

Eva ran away inside, and she would not come out.

Her adoptive mother said, "What are you saying? Her mother is dead. She was taken in a collection."

"We've got a letter from Kharpert, and we're taking her."

But Eva hid and wouldn't go. Three times we sent someone, and three times she refused to go anywhere.

So, I said, "Artapart, if you know any workers who are good, send me to them so I can go. I am either going to die right here or go to find my children. This is no life for me."[121]

He sent word to those on a supply caravan. The head, a Turkish merchant, said to me, "I'll take you as my sister as long as you don't go as an Armenian. I'm going to get a paper from a general that this soldier is in Mardin in the hospital, and you are his wife who wants to go to him." He gave this information from his mouth and my mouth to the Turkish officials.[122] When they gave me the paper, it made me secure. That paper had a lot of respect.

So, I am going as the Turkish soldier's wife. When I was preparing to leave, an Armenian woman named Altoun ran to me and said, "My son is over there. I was deported to Syria and had to walk all over. I found out my child is there. How can I bring him? What can I do? Take me!"

They put her with me as my servant. I covered myself with Turkish shawls and got on my horse. I had done all this secretly so the local Turks would not recognize me.

I looked to see that *Effendi* who had hated me running down in his bathrobe!

"Guleeg, where are you going!"

"I'm going with these people to bring my children."

He wrote a paper to the workers. He said, "I'm giving you some names. Any *Tademtzi* who says, bring me back, bring them." One name he gave was a Luseeg, in Dikranogerd.[123]

In my mind, I was saying, "He's fooling me. He gave them a paper to kill me." But, it is four years later, and the orders are over.

We started out on the road. Then that *Hadji Agha*, the one that I smashed all the windows on, shouldn't he come across me!

"Guleeg!" he called.

I said nothing.

Softly he came near; he drove his horse near. "Do you think if you don't talk, I won't recognize you?"

"*Hadji Agha*," I said. "Shut your mouth. Don't say a word. There is news of Eva. I'm going to go and fetch her."

He said, "Go very carefully. Don't sleep at night. Don't trust yourself to those."

"I didn't trust myself to you," I said. "I am just biting my soul and going."

I was 34 years old at that time. It was the time of my youth. I had strength. We started out, on the road. We went long; we went short.

On the way, wherever and whenever we were going to sleep, the merchant would start a fire. It's hot in Syria! Every night, we would stay on a hill and keep watch. He would say, "When you sleep, I'll look out. When I sleep, you look out. The road around here is a criminal nest. And I don't trust these workers."

One day we reached as far as Ichme. It was dark.

"We're going to sleep here," he said.

In that town, there was a Turk, an *Effendi,* who knew Hagop from the village. This man was bringing goods to Ichme because there was no cotton, nothing. Whatever they needed, he bought and hired someone to cart.

I said to the others, "Don't say there's anyone here from Kharpert to that man. He's a very evil man. That man had a gang, and he was the official of them."

He came over and saw me, "Sister, I can speak Armenian. You can talk freely. I understand." He had married an Armenian wife before. "I'll take you to her, and we can go see the church."

"No, I'm too tired." I was afraid he would slay me, for when he had married that Armenian wife in Tadem, he had beat her. Her mother had come to Hagop, and he had gone with the mother and beat him.

The workers said to us, "At least go and get a drink of water from the spring. It's beautiful, clear water."

We cautiously walked, took a drink, and cautiously returned. I knew the place of an Armenian there who lived on a Kurd's property. He had saved two women; these women had escaped on the road somewhere, and he had taken pity and brought them to live in his small barn. They worked for him. The Kurd was kind to them.

Oh, Lord, when we came to those women, it was as if they saw a light! They were so happy!

We stayed the night there.

Then we went. We went and went. We travelled a lot; we travelled a little. We reached Dikranogerd[124] where there are four walls. It was told, in the greatest time of the Armenians, an Armenian king Dikran had built it, and his queen Dikranouhi would sit atop.

The head of the supply caravan got a telegram as soon as he entered: "Don't come. The English have surrounded Mardin."

He said, "Either I have to leave the supplies in Dikranogerd, or I am going to have to return them."

I said to him, "I won't go back. If you go, go. Only I'll tell you a letter to write from me to my sister that you took me as far as Dikranogerd."

We walked into the town. We are still in shawls; we are Turkish *kha-nums*. Suddenly I heard church bells. I know that Turks do not ring church bells, so I took Altoun in that direction. The church turned out to be Syrian. I gave them the address of the Miaseen *Bey*[125]—where that Luseeg was—and the Syrians took us.

We knocked on the door. Oh! A dog that is God almighty tall!

A girl came and pulled the dog into a barn. She came back to the peephole and said, "Who are you? What do you want?" in Turkish.

"My sister Luseeg is here." I said 'sister' so they would let us in. She was a woman I had met at a farm, and I made her a sister.[126]

She called out, "Luseeg! Your sister's come!"

Luseeg came, and I told her, "I said you were my sister. Don't make me a liar."

She said, "You're more than my sister."

I slept one night at her house. Luseeg would not let us go out. Her Turk's house was huge! He was very, very rich.

I said, "Never mind all this. You get ready. When we come back, we're going to take you."

"I'm ready," she said. "I just work and live, and they say when the roads are open, I can go to America."

When we woke in the morning, she wanted us to give us a note to the person who had separated her from the convoy and was in Mardin now.

I refused: "No, don't give us any letter."

We stood outside. Altoun said, "I know the road to Mardin. We'll go by ourselves."

We walked and walked. Our shoes became torn apart. We were barefoot, bareheaded. The rain began pouring. We got soaked from head to toe. We slept behind big stones. We walked and walked.

We lay down at the side of a village and looked around. I saw the son of an old Kurdish neighbor standing there. When his mother had become a war refugee in Kharpert, I used to take good care of her. She used to bring blood from Mezre, and I would cook it in the ovens so that it became like a liver,[127] and she and her son could eat it.

Along the journey, Altoun and I wanted to stay as strangers; we were veiled, head to toe. Now, we had no choice. We were desperate and had to go to some place. What were we going to do? We had to ask him.

I said, "Child, where is the inn?"

"It rained and rained, and this place's inn collapsed."

"Well, where can visitors stay?"

"I have only a mother. Give us the inn money, and you can sleep with us."

What were we going to do? We went.

There was no light. They were burning the pines as a fire, and that was the light. The water was falling off us.

He said in their tongue, "These were two journeyers. I told them this and brought them."

"All right, *khanum*," his mother said, and took my shawl off. When she saw me, she said, "*Ooooeeeee!*" and hugged me. "This place is the Bloody Village. Any saved Armenians they take and slay. There is no witness or protector for the Armenians! My son did well to bring you here. They would kill you whether you had 12 cents or what. It's a horrible place."

That night we slept on the floor. She dried us, gave us a blanket, and kept us warm. I asked her whether there was a government in this place. She said there was only one official. I put on all my shawls and asked that her son take me to that *Effendi* but not to say we were Armenians.

I said, "Come, Altoun. We will either be killed, or we will lie and save ourselves."

It was ten o'clock in the morning, and the guard was standing there at the door. I asked in Turkish, "Is the *Bey Effendi* still asleep, or is he up?"

The guard checked and said, "He's drinking his morning coffee." After a while, he went back and asked; the official said, 'Whoever it is, let them come.'"

He said to us, "What do you want, my dears?"

I replied, "My husband is in Mardin, sick in the hospital, and our driver's horse's leg broke; he went to fix things and hasn't come back. Give me security so I can go safely to Mardin's hospital. I want to make it in time."

He rubbed and rubbed his beard. He said, "How can I give you protection? They ate and finished the Armenians. Now the Turks and Arabs are killing each other. I sent 30 soldiers out and two returned. They went to help someone, and they were all killed but two. They ate the rest. This is a wild place…. There are supply caravans. Perhaps I can arrange for you to go with them."

"No. We have no place or food. Where will we stay?" (I said to myself, "Oh Lord, he's smelling our Armenian odors! They will sell us as slaves."[128]) "We'll go and think about it."

We went out, and there were two men on horseback pulling two donkeys without loads. I said, "Run, Altoun."

"What about our belongings?" she said.

"Never mind them. Run. We have to get out of here and save our lives."

We ran up, and I grabbed the reins.[129]

"What do you want?"

"Won't you take us? Our driver's horse broke its leg. He went away and hasn't come back."

"We'll take you, but we will take for one piece of gold each."

I paid them two pieces of gold to go. I said to Altoun, "Don't say a word. If they find out we're Armenian, it is very bad." We went with them, still as Turks, to Mardin. One of the men had married an Armenian girl, but we gave no recognition of any kind. Even underneath, I am wrapped like the Turks are, so if they grab my shawl, I'm still a *namaran*, the Turkish lady no one sees.[130]

We rode little; we rode lot.

One day remained to reach Mardin. The two men were stopping off for the night at a big inn. When we entered the inn, we found the place filled with soldiers! The war was over. The Germans had made peace. The Turks and Germans were pulling their soldiers back.

The two who brought us said, "This is where we stay. You go to a corner and stay there. Don't sleep tonight."

I won't sleep! I will sit here, and the soldiers will sit over there! How can it be this way? Supposing—on account of us—they start a fight, and the two men are killed? What will we do? I thought and thought and thought. Finally, I asked if there was an owner of another inn?

One man said, "Yes, just a small one. His house is above."

"Call him to me."

He came and I said, "I'm the wife of a general. He's sick, and I'm going to Mardin for him. I do not want to stay in the midst of these soldiers. Bring me to your house if you are a family."

"I'm a family. You're welcome to come."

The man gathered us, and we went. What privileges and respect! The bread, the honey! They dried us, fed us, and had us drink. They brought a wonderful mattress for each one of us. We were going to rest! The room is like a parlor, but much bigger. Whatever orphans there are, this man has gathered.

I heard Altoun say, "My aunt's child! My aunt's child!"

I said, "Altoun, we came as Turks!"

In my mind it was coming that, with all the Red Cross workers, we could now come back, freely, as Armenians and pick the child up. "Please do not say anything. I beg of you."

She called the girl over. Altoun knew Kurdish because she had remained a long time with the Kurds. She said, "Turkish or Kurdish?"

The girl said, "I'm Kurdish."

"Oh, my god, they've made my child a Kurd. This is my house's child!"[131]

I convinced Altoun we could reclaim the girl by coming back with Red Cross workers. Then we won't even have to come with shawls.

In the morning, the two men came for us. "Come on, *Khanum*."

Mardin was circular. I could not wait to set foot in that city! But I'm not familiar with the place. Where is the Red Cross? If I knew, I would get off there.

Altoun said, "We can go to the hospital." There were people she knew there. Her sister-in-law, who had escaped, was there. It turned out my neighbor was also there, but where was the hospital?

We saw a Catholic priest and asked the way. He yelled in Turkish, "Those Illuminator faces![132] Where are you going! Walking! Walking! The sky has fallen! Because of you the world was destroyed! Get the hell out of here!"

We went by and walked a little more. Whoever's door we knocked on, they would not open it. Finally, we saw this man. A cultured man's walk is recognizable. I said, "The Turks have eaten us, but we may come across a good one. Let's ask him."

I cut in front of him and asked the way. It happened he was a big doctor in the hospital. He said, "What do you want to know?"

We were Armenians now. I said, "My sister is there." I was still hoping to find Marnos and her baby.

Altoun added, "My sister-in-law is there."

He said, "Come, dear ones." It happened that her sister-in-law was the one who made all the meals for the hospital. These nurses had separated the Armenian orphans and were nursing them.

That doctor walked a mile with us to bring us to the hospital. As soon as he entered the hospital, he called out, "Quick! There are people come from Kharpert. They are soaked from the rain and almost dying. Change them from head to toe and feed them. Their stomachs hurt." He was a good man.

All the Armenians gathered around: Who's alive? Who's alive! This one's alive; that one's alive! There is one from our village. Also, Mamas, Jooar, Sharistanuh. They took us inside, bathed, changed us, and put us to bed.

I kept calling out, "Jooar! Jooar! Have you seen my Eva?"

"Yes, I see her. I see her, my dear."

Mamas added, "She talks and runs away. She introduces herself and runs away."

That night, we slept there. In the morning, I rose and said to Mamas, our neighbor, "Do you know this government?"

"Yes."

"Get in front of me. I'm going to the government. I can't go on a guess. I can't guess which house is Eva's."

I had my name written by the writer there, and he went to the Director. There were masses of people. He called me first. I was amazed.

"My dear," he said. "I'm *Kharpetzi*. What do you want?"

"I want my daughter."

"What is her name?"

I told him, her Armenian name is this, her age is this.

He called a big man, Naphar, who said, "I know her. She's in a rich place. Do you think she'd want to come with you? Do you want me to take you there?" He was Eva's adoptive mother's brother!

Mamas said, "There's a Yegheki girl, Naomi, who knows that place."

"Let's go," I said.

We started out and went to Naomi's house. She used to come and play with Eva in Yegheki. When she saw us coming, she ran away from fear. She went to call her foster mother, who asked, "What do you want?"

"That girl knows where my daughter is, and I want you to send her with me to show me the way."

She scolded Naomi, "Why did you run away? They want you. Come on." That family had saved the girl. She was a soul, and they were keeping her. There are many nice people.

As soon as Naomi came back, she said, "Mary is dead."

I made one scream and cried, "*Vak!* Child! Child! I'm not going to see you again!" I cried and cried.

Her *khanum* said, "Don't go up. Just show the door and come back. They're important people, and they'll break from us."

Naomi didn't mind. As soon as she reached the house, she ran up. Eva had dressed and primped and was going down to the stores.

I hugged her and cried. "*Yavroos*. Sweetheart," I said, "There were three of you, and only you are left."

Her adoptive mother came out. "Shofkeeah, who is it?"

"My mother."

"You told me she was dead."

"I thought she was, but she's alive."

We went in and talked... I did not stay too long. I did not say too much.... Eva sat beside me a little, but then she went to her adoptive mother, rubbed her back, and looked after her.

[Long Pause]

I thought, When I get to know some people and find a place then I will take Eva with me.... Wherever I went or walked, I came back to them.

I told them I was looking for my sister, Marnos.

During this wait, I would go to the government and tell them, an Armenian person is in this place, and I'm going to get this boy, that girl. I would bring our survivors to the Red Cross headquarters....[133]

... I saw our Toros. Boghosian. A sack on him and all over his body, sores. He was in a hug position, sitting in the street. He was six or seven years old.

"Toros?" I said.

He looked. "*Ahaaeeee.*"

"Come," I said. "I'm taking you to the American Red Cross." He had no one. The family had all been massacred. The Americans came and examined him, and they separated him, all sores, into a room. When I got up in the morning, he had run away.[134]

.... There was a bride in another city. I went. I took a government official, got her out, and brought her.

.... Melkon I saved from the village.[135]

We put them all together in the Red Cross, which had soldier-doctors who were Armenian ....

.... Finally, they said this would be the last train that could take us out.

"All right," I said to Eva, "we are going."

Her adoptive mother asked, "What does she want?"

Eva said, "We're going."

Her adoptive mother insisted her husband, working in the government, come. He came because they told him how his wife was shrieking and crying. She had been good to Eva. She was a nice woman.

She cried and screamed! She had no children of her own.

Her husband said, "It's no use. That's the law."

I had made sure to appeal to the government.[136] He called his servant and told him to fetch bread from the oven and carry it with us until we reached the Red Cross. He took out two pieces of gold and gave them to us.

We went to the American Red Cross and that station where the Armenian soldier-doctors told us would be the final train. In one car, there were Armenian girls that Turkish soldiers had taken and married, the pretty ones. The Armenian doctors told me, "We will sit on the train in the other car with their husbands. You sit with these girls and persuade them…." He confided in me that the brides' wagon was going to Aleppo, but the soldiers' wagon would go to Adana, so they won't see each other.[137]

"You take care of the brides," he told me.

Now we were on the train, and I was talking and talking and persuading the brides. They're crying and screaming. "Where is the *Effendi*? They saved our lives! They fed us rice pilaf! We were starving! They gave us nice clothes! *Effendi! Effendi!*"[138]

Our train wagon arrived in Aleppo. At the station were all the English, who had taken over Aleppo. Doctor Garo called the guard and sent a message, "I got rid of my load. You bring your load to me." He took care of the girls.[139]

One Marzbed heard I was in Aleppo and called me. He knew me. He was my age, and in the village, we used to play together as children. "My dearest," he said, "where are your people? What are you eating?"

I said, "Marzbed, what are we to eat?"

He said, "Sweet, let your daughter stay with me. Here, she can eat, sleep. I'll give her clothes." He was in a Catholic building.

"Eva, will you stay?"

"Yes, I'll stay."

When she lived there, they made her pray a lot, hours, and she didn't know their language. Eva stayed a month or two. Then she said, "There's an Armenian church where a school has started. I will go there."

Meanwhile I went to the Consul, and he told me he would notify my husband. His wife lived in New York, and she put it in the Armenian papers in America that Hagop Haroian's wife and daughter are in Aleppo and need money. He did me that favor.

Hagop sent $300 and said, "Send them to me."

Well, he was not a citizen, and the American door was not open to Armenians. He had his first papers.

He said, "If you don't send them, I'm going to come."

But they wouldn't allow those that weren't citizens in, so what to do?

The interpreter at the Consulate was Armenian. One Buzmushentzi Moosegh went with me to see him and said, "I knew this woman's husband. He devoted his life to the cause. Help him. Help her."

The interpreter said to me, "You don't know how to read and write? Well, on this day, the Consul is going on vacation. You come then."

The Consul went on vacation. I got up and went. The interpreter held my hand and guided it to sign my passport. He said, "When you're on the train, learn how to write your name. If you don't, when you get to France, they'll send you back."

We started the journey. There was an Armenian woman from Aleppo with us. We had paid for her because she had sent word to her husband, who had not answered, but she had already taken out her passport.

Eva said, "Mother, our money is a lot. Let's give her some, so she can buy her ticket."

That day, three ships sailed. They tipped and tipped and tipped. The other two ships capsized.

We passed Beirut, and then sailed to France, where they examined us. There was an Istanbul Hotel with many Armenians, where I stayed 15 days until the boat passage to America was arranged.

On the boat from Paris,[140] I was seasick. I grew so sick that the sailors brought an interpreter to ask for my address, possessions, and money to send to my husband because they thought I was going to die. They had put me in the sickroom. An Armenian girl, Akabee, who understood French well, came and told me, "They said they're going to bury you at sea."

They gave me nothing to eat. Later, I thought, "All right, I'm going to die. The milk is over there, the ice is over there, but they won't give them to me." So, when the nurses went to sleep, I got up. I drank the milk, ate the ice, then came back and slept. By the time the nurse stirred, I had finished them. I thought, "They're going to throw me in the water. Why can't I have something to eat?"

Morning finally dawned…. They brought my clothes. Akabee returned: "Get up, Mama. We are in New York."

"They were supposed to throw me in the sea!"

"That's what they said. It's a good thing it didn't happen."

The officials took us into the examining place. An American was holding an Armenian paper. The interpreter, an Armenian, asked me if I knew how to read and write.

I said, "I knew a little, but I've forgotten from the shock of the deportations."

"Well, just say a Lord's Prayer."

"No! I can recite letters. 'A, b, c….'"

He said, "Your husband has written me a letter. Go stand over there near the Red Cross. We are going to put you on the train."

I was so tired. I didn't want to go anywhere.

I said, "I want to sleep one night in New York."

I didn't want to go near the Red Cross anymore. Let them stay where they are. I was going to a hotel.

That woman that I brought with us, and every one of hers surrounded me. They said, "We'll put you on the train. It will take you straight to Waukegan!"

So, we stayed a night in the hotel, and they came in the morning and put us on the train straight to Waukegan. I knew no English. Eva didn't either. We sat, and at each stop, Eva jumped up and shouted, "Waukegan?"

The conductor said, "Stay there, stay there."

We went long; we went little.[141]

When we arrived in Chicago, they put us on another train.

Then that train stopped. Eva said, "Tonight we have to stay here. Where can we go?"

"Let's go up the hill," I said. "I see a light, and I will ask where we are."

I went and showed the address I had to an old man.

"Hurry up!" he cried. "Your bus is leaving." He grabbed us and put us on the bus.

There was an Armenian man, just come out of the hospital, sitting near us. All the way there, he never said he was Armenian.

Then, when the stop came, he said, "Get off, mother, at our stop."

I said, "Who are you?"

He replied, "I am God's servant."

"The whole world is God's servant."

"Get off," he replied. "I know your people. Get off, and I will take you."

"If you don't give me your name, I won't take a step," I said. There was a lot of money with us.

"See that store? Where there is a light? Your address is there. I'm taking you there."

Eva said, "Come on, Mama. Let's get off and go. He's only one. We are two."

"Yes, but what if we go there and they become four?"

"No, no," the man said. He took an oath and took us where the light was.

It was our Uncle Peter's Sarkis' store. In New York, Eva and I had bought such hats and clothes! Sarkis had never seen us that way. As soon as I walked in, he said, "Hey, here come the Indians."

They surrounded us. Then they took us to the house of our friend, Sareeg der Bedrosian, who could take us to Hagop's. She hugged me.

I said, "Sareeg, your mother and father are not here. Let me rest for a while." I rested in quiet.

Then I said, "I want to go home."

She took us to Papa's house, but he wasn't there.

Hagop had heard whisperings about the capsized ships, and he had gone to find any news. He had been saying, "If they are dead, tell me!"

Some people made a mistake and wrote from Beirut that Guleeg's boat was one of two that had tipped over!

When we entered, Uncle Boghos was there. He hugged Eva. Paylazeen and Nersus hugged me.

"*Mayrus! Hayrus!*" They called out to their mother and father.

"Let me be," I said. "Let me sit."

From that sea of blood, what I have told is just a drop.

BONES AND BODIES, WE HAD TO WALK OVER THEM

EVA HIGHTAIAN (née HAROIAN)

Edited by Gil Harootunian, PhD
Afterword by Rebecca Jinks

Editor's Introduction:
"Bones and Bodies, We Had to Walk over Them...."

Barely a nine-year-old child in 1915, Eva Hightaian (née Haroian) survived the Genocide through forced transfer into a Muslim household. She was deported from her village of Tadem, and she lost two sisters, Mary, aged 11, and Elizabeth, aged 4, who had been rounded up in the same collection. A maternal aunt who was on the same deportation helped Eva and her older sister Mary stay alive until they reached the city of Mardin, further south and largely populated by Syrian Arabs. Aunt Marnos had been pressuring the two girls to save themselves. Mary heeded the advice when she could not walk any more. Eva heeded the advice shortly after, and never saw that aunt again. Eva survived and provided this oral history on the collections in Tadem, the Death March, and her forced transfer into an Arab household. Within Eva's story are two more stories—the stories of Elizabeth and Mary, her sisters who did not survive.

As Eva began to deliver her oral history, in those first few moments, she paused and asked questions about the tape recorder, which troubled her. I was also surprised to hear for the first time a phenomenal woman like my Aunt Eva express doubt about the value of a story about herself. My mother and I needed to give her affirmation of how important her history was. My Aunt Eva composed herself—and delivered her full story. As Eva concludes her oral history, she states with firmness:

"And now the Turks claim they never did such a thing. But I saw it with my own eyes, in my young days, my childhood, they did all those things…. That is the life we went through. That's the life I want to tell you about in Tadem. Tadem was a group, an Armenian community, and that is where I was born. I am Eva Hightaian. I am married now. I was Haroian before. I remember my young days."

As Eva was delivering her oral history to me, her niece, and to her younger sister Rose, some conversational exchanges took place. Some were included in this oral history if the exchange enhanced its meaning. For example, the first time Eva mentioned her grandmother, her younger sister Rose interrupts with eagerness to learn the name of her grandmother. This exchange is included to illustrate the depths that survivors buried their nightmare. Local killers will murder savagely the grandmother of Eva—and of Rose—during the Genocide. Rose was born in America and found crushing silence instead of family stories.

Scholars have increasingly acknowledged the importance of child transfer in genocides. Watenpaugh notes child transfer is an integral component of genocide, requiring "an immense political project" and "requisite bureaucratic measures needed to facilitate it in practice" (2013, page 290). He argues: "Any agenda for future research on the genocide must re-center children—as more than just young victims of murder but also as the embodiment of social capital, culture, and belonging, and as tools for perpetrator social engineering and objects of intense interests in the rebuilding of diasporan and survivor communities" (Watenpaugh, 2013, page 294).

Selva when discussing child transfer notes the human rights approach can rewrite "the voiceless back into the historical narratives by disentangling them from dominant narratives of larger institutions and nation states," and this can provide "the nuance and dignity" that the survivors' stories deserve (Selva, 2019, page 58). Darbinyan too has discussed how such work allows for "a more nuanced picture of the Armenian refugees, in contrast to the homogenous and faceless 'waves' of people described in most reports prepared by the relief organizations or government agencies" (2020, page 26). Selva has argued the need for "a reconsideration of traditional narratives of the genocide that failed to acknowledge them [children]. This implores a unique methodological approach of centering children and their active positions in the narratives of the genocide" (Selva, 2019, page 57). Finally, Maksudyan's body of scholarship is a testament to how much more nuanced an understanding we can gain of child survivors by studying distinctly their experiences (2019).

Eva's oral history is significant in many ways because it reveals the decision-making process of a nine-year-old child as she experiences the collections, the Death March, and forced transfer into a Muslim household. Eva initially resists deportation. The first time Eva is collected for a deportation, she follows her mother's instructions to escape. The second time that perpetrators grab Eva for a collection, Eva observes one Turkish soldier who is highly decorated yet calm and thoughtful looking. Eva makes her way over to that soldier, tells him that her mother is married to a Turkish soldier (i.e., a convert to Islam), and that she and her little sister were grabbed while playing. The soldier confirms this with a local Turk, and then asks the local Turk to take the two girls to their mother. On the road, Eva waits until she reaches the exact place where her Aunt Takouhi passes each day as she carts flour for the Ottoman Army troops. Eva politely excuses herself from the old Turk who is escorting her and her little sister. She waits, alone and patient, for her Aunt Takouhi. Her aunt finally arrives, and Eva reaches home in the safety of her Aunt Takouhi and, in doing so, and makes sure her little sister Elizabeth reaches home with her. More weeks of hiding and fear follow, and when Eva is collected for a third time, she no longer makes an effort to save herself.

At the third collection site, one of the first instructions that Aunt Marnos gives Eva and Mary is to mess their hair and dirty their faces and clothes to avoid rape and to avoid abduction into a Muslim household (Hightaian, Personal Interview). The tactic of making themselves unattractive to Muslim abductors indicates their initial decision was to survive the deportation with their Armenian identity intact. Sarafian notes the Death Marches were a means to weaken the young women and children by isolating and then terrorizing them (2010, page 210). Eva's history shows how that policy worked on the individual level. Families may have set out with a tenacious will to stay Armenian. The starvation, dehydration, and disease, as well as the viciousness of the Death Squads (Çetes), on the Death Marches, forced many women and children to into the life-or-death option to transfer into Muslim households.

After Eva's transfer to a Muslim household, she narrates her years with an Arab adoptive mother. The Arab family erases Eva's Armenian identity: she converts to Islam, is given the name Shofkeeah,[142] and is forbidden to speak Armenian or even tell anyone that she is Armenian. That did not stop members of the Muslim household, however, from periodically reminding Eva that she was born an infidel.[143]

Three years pass, and the Allied Forces are victorious. They support the Armenians to reclaim those taken from Muslim households. Guleeg Haroian discovers Eva is alive and goes to Mardin to reclaim her. Eva then narrates her struggle to decide whether to go with her mother or to remain with her Arab adoptive mother. Eva makes the decision to go with her mother, Guleeg Haroian, and in 1920, Eva arrives in America with her mother to join her father, Hagop Haroian.

Yet, Eva is hesitant to leave her Arab adoptive mother, and this reluctance highlights the painful struggle of some captured orphans and brides to decide whether to remain in their Muslim homes or to return to the Armenian community. The reasons for their struggle are many. For the first reason, Eva is precise: "I'm not going back to the old country with you. I don't want to be the way I was there…." Eva fears the cold, near-starvation, and chronic abuse by Turkish and Kurdish overlords that she experienced throughout her childhood in Tadem, an experience that culminated in the arrests, torture, murders, gang rapes, and Death Marches of the 1915

Genocide.[144] "Terror" may be the word to describe the source of Eva's reluctance to rejoin the Armenian community. The Ottoman Empire terrorized its Armenian citizens. Tachjian observes on reclaimed females: "...the person concerned was still traumatized as a result of her experiences, and was not convinced that times had changed" (2009, page 73). A missionary who had been reared in the Ottoman Empire described the impact on the "reign of terror" in Armenia: "On the whole, the same condition of alarm prevails among the Armenians as I witnessed previously among the Syrian *rayahs*.[145] It is more than alarm—it is abject terror, and not without good reason" (1896, pages 285-286). Kaloosdian notes that Tademtzis during the 1915 Genocide "lived in constant fright, horror, and disbelief" (2015, page 66). For three years, Eva had lived in safety and in luxury in her Arab adoptive mother's home. She leaves because she has a safe escape route: her father Hagop Haroian is in America.[146]

The second reason for Eva's hesitancy to re-join her mother and the Armenian community lies in Eva's perspective of a nine-year-old child. For instance, Guleeg Haroian attributes the horrors of the Genocide to the Turkish[147] perpetrators and seeks information to help her and her children survive their reign of horror:

> "I decided to find out whether this was government law or the evil of the village Turks who, over the years, had done killings. But the Turkish police had surrounded the village; no one could leave. Whoever tried to escape, they'd catch. I had to duck out of the village. Anna and I hurried to the Vali in Mezre because the Vali's wagoneer was my in-law.
>
> I went in and said, "The village is in this situation. What's going to happen?"

Eva understands that the Turks are doing 'bad things' (a nine-year-old's vocabulary). Her overriding emotion is a "hunger" (Hightaian, Personal Interview) for her mother after she is grabbed in a collection: she wants her mother to come and repeatedly comments that her mother did not come.

Her comments are those of a child who has not matured enough to assign blame to the perpetrators of the Genocide and the perpetrators alone. One of the most painful moments comes when Eva blames herself for the loss of her four-year-old sister Elizabeth on the Death March. At another point, Eva blames her mother Guleeg for the death of her older sister Mary. Eva like all children had once seen her mother as god-like, but she had that belief ripped from her when her mother could not save them. Worse, Eva saw her mother brutalized right in front of her, that night in the first collection. Finally, when Eva's mother locates her in Mardin and makes an appeal to the government for her repatriation, Eva provides insights on her personal struggle as an adolescent but makes no mention of the legal struggle taking place in the adult courts.

The third reason for Eva's reluctance to re-join the Armenian community is the extent to which Eva—like many hostages—identified with her Muslim captors. She complains that her mother Guleeg did not allow her to speak Arabic and purposefully sold all of Eva's Arab belongings: "My mother made me a *dhimmi.*" A *dhimmi*—the Muslim word for the infidels over whom they ruled, viciously. Scholars have noted many children or young brides who had the fortune to transfer into kinder Muslim households ended up bonding to their new families. Eva clearly bonds with her kind Arab mother. Yet, by disparaging Armenians as *dhimmi*, Eva clearly shows signs of another condition that specialists had not yet identified, much less designed a course of treatment: Stockholm syndrome. Experiencing forced identification with oppressors is a distinct emotional issue, related to but different from bonding.

The Ottoman authorities had terrorized the Armenians for years, and when the *vorpahavak* (collection of orphans) began, resistance from the Muslim captors was strong. Current estimates are that fewer than 20,000 out of the 100,000-200,000 Armenians who had undergone forced transfer were collected, and "some areas never yielded a single Armenian woman or child" (Sarafian, 2010, page 217). In short, the Armenians were hostages in the Ottoman Empire. Eva's statement—"My mother made me a *dhimmi*"—impresses upon readers the political will of the Young Turks to force on children "at an impressionable and receptive age a culture and mentality different from their parents" (Abtahi and Web, 2008, 1:235, cited in Watenpaugh, 2013, page 288). The indoctrination was thorough, relentless, and brutal. In the Genocide, gone was "the child's right to identity or other categories of rights" including belonging to his or her "natal group" (Watenpaugh, 2013, page 288). Selna reinforces that the Death Marches and Death Camps were important factors allowing the Ottoman authorities to manipulate and reconstruct the identity of the children (2019, page 60) and delineates how the Ottoman orphanages were sites of "cultural genocide" (2019, page 63).

One American humanitarian worker gives a description of the indoctrination of children that aligns with the definition of Stockholm syndrome that specialists will write decades later:

> In a letter dated to July 16, 1921 and addressed to the secretary general of the League of Nations, Emma D. Cushman, an American humanitarian worker from Near East Relief (NER), estimated that some 6,000 Armenians in Constantinople and 60,000 Armenian children remained in captivity. She remarked on the unique and clever manner in which the Turks contrive to conceal the identity of the children. They try to bring about not so much a change a [sic] name and locality, but rather a complete change of mind in the child. These children, for a period of time extending from one week to three months, will deny strenuously that they are christians. Some indeed will go so far to revile the christians as infidels, and declare they are loyal Moslems, while at the same time their history is sufficiently doubtful to keep them under observation, and sooner or later will be forthcoming that they are indeed Christians. (Manuk-Khaloyan, n.d., page 5; *see also* page 6)

The fourth and final reason for Eva's hesitation to go with her mother Guleeg Haroian is Eva's strong agency. Maksudyan notes that *jarbig* is a frequent descriptor for child survivors but that *jarbig* is a stand-in term for "agency." She cautions readers about the real meaning of "agency" during the Genocide:

> *The emphasis on children's agency should, however, be not read as an idealization, in which resilience and survival are direct outcomes of agency. My focus on agency is definitely not because it necessarily leads to survival, but because it challenges the victim narrative. Armenian children survived under paradoxical circumstances. They were definitely targets (and so, victims) of direct violence, sexual exploitation, and erasure of their identities. They were also agents who tried to fight back through escape, pretension, and resistance. In this context, their agency should not be seen as limitless, or one that could bring progressive change. Agency, in that picture, was mostly the capacity to endure and suffer." (Maksudyan 2019, pages 21-22)*

Like her mother Guleeg who endures, like her Aunt Marnos who saves her on the Death March, and like her older sister Mary who works for her captors for years only to be pushed out and have to brave a long walk, alone, to the big city to find food, Eva too has determined to survive. Eva's struggle four years after the Genocide is how best to do this. Other child survivors show similar agency: for example, one child survivor leaves his re-found mother to take an exciting train ride and "embark on new adventures in a new city by the sea" (Maksudyan, 2010, pages 27-28). This child and his mother had undergone separation for four years. Similarly, Eva had survived the Death Marches as a nine-year-old child, and her mother came to reclaim Eva when she was a thirteen-year-old adolescent.

Eva Hightaian's oral history also provides one final insight into another female on the Death March: her Aunt Marnos. Her Aunt Marnos is determined to survive the tragedy and to save any children she can. Aunt Marnos obtains food for Eva and her sisters through trading her high-quality white clothing, clothing which was finite and must have been running out fast. Moreover, Aunt Marnos provides this care though she herself must have been in primal shock at having to abandon her own infant and, doubtless, at being raped in the nightly orgies of the Death Marches. Eva states that Aunt Marnos keeps telling her that if she saves herself (i.e., transfers into a Muslim household), then she, Aunt Marnos, may be able to save herself, too: *Aunt Marnos is persisting in the Death March only for her nieces.* Her advice saves Eva's life. Those who remained in the Death Marches were driven south, with more and more dying on the way, until the deportees reached the desert concentration camps where they were killed in batches or left to die a slow and agonizing death. To Eva, Aunt Marnos' advice may have felt like abandonment, yet Eva states: "And so I lived."

All three Haroian survivors—Eva, her mother Guleeg, and her uncle Bedros Haroian—experienced the deepest trauma. The trauma persisted for decades, especially as medical specialists had neither identified their condition nor made available treatment:

> *Haroian cannot escape the past's trauma, however. When he begins with enthusiasm his travel to join the Russian Army in Transcausia, he has to re-cross the Keotur Bridge, that scene of slaughter. The scene reveals Bedros Haroian has a condition that will neither be identified nor have effective treatments until 1980: Post-Traumatic Stress Syndrome. His PTSD includes adrenaline rushes and high definition images.... (Haroian, 2021, page xvii).*

The disruption of the primal bond between mother and child is inconsolable, and Guleeg Haroian experienced this disruption *four* times—as a child, her father was murdered; as an adult, her two children Elizabeth and Mary were murdered and her mother Vartouhi was savagely murdered. Guleeg also experienced mass trauma twice—the 1895 Great Massacres and the 1915 Genocide.

Trauma affects each person in a different way. Both Guleeg Haroian and Eva Hightaian experienced nightmares for decades post-Genocide.[148]

Guleeg Haroian's nightmares never ended. Guleeg Haroian was my maternal grandmother, and as a child I lived in an extended family household with her. I would hear her shouts as a nightmare awoke her during the night and even during the day if for a moment she dozed off. Despite the trauma, however, my grandmother welcomed every opportunity to chronicle her experiences and bear witness to the Genocide. Guleeg never stopped believing in fighting for justice; she wanted the injustice recorded and published. Eva Hightaian (née Haroian) went through the Genocide as a child. Her nightmares lessened with time. After I recorded Eva's oral history and the follow up interview, however, the nightmares came back, or, rather, the one nightmare that dominated swam up from the depths of Eva's mind: her younger sister crying out, "Eva, don't leave me! Eva! Where are you? I want my mother! I want my sisters! Eva, don't leave me!" Eva told me of the new recurrence of the nightmare to explain why she would no longer discuss her experiences during the Genocide with me. Eva documented her experiences, and then she re-focused on the present.

Note: *[Pause]* indicates a moment that was so distressing that Eva Hightaian had to stop for a few moments and collect herself.

"Bones and Bodies, We Had to Walk over Them"
by Eva Hightaian (née Haroian)

When I was six years old, my father was coming back from the United States to visit the village for a while.[149] I ran a couple of miles where they came near to the village. My father saw me, hugged me, put me on his shoulder, and we walked home to the village together. When we came, mother and Mary were waiting for us, and my grandmother, too. All the village people were waiting because their sons and fathers were coming. Everybody took their own family to their houses, and they had feasts, and they were happy, kissing each other. Their sons had come! That was the greatest happiness of their life, in the little Tadem, the village where I was born.

Mother and father, and our grandmother, we lived together. I was six, and Mary was about seven and a half years old. A year later, we had Elizabeth, another baby.

[Rose interrupts: What was grandmother's name?[150]

Eva response: Vartouhi.][151]

Father bought a white horse two weeks later. When we used to go to the fields to work, my father put my mother back of him on the horse, and they used to ride! Everybody was jealous! He used to put his wife right on the horse! We were so happy.

My father was a guard at the village. He used to guard all the land, the grapes and all that. He was a very brave man.

When he lived a year with us, a cattle drive, going place to place to sell, came. The men were working in the fields. All the women and children were near the brook. This cattle drive rushes in! These Arabs do not care! All the clothes the women washed and lay on the grass! The women take all the children, like a picnic. The men worked in the fields or in the village. This *Rawhide*[152] comes right there. Hundreds and hundreds of cattle go right into the village! All the women, the children were frightened. They didn't know where to run so they'd be alive! The children were trapped between the cows! The village women were crying, yelling.

No one, no man, went near them. Somebody ran to my father: "Hagop! Hagop! A cattle drive is here! They're killing all the children and the women down at the brook!"

My father says, "Why? Where are all the men?"

They had all run into their houses and closed their doors. Nobody comes out.

So my father sees a wagon that we put the hay in and bring from the fields. He pulled the whole side off the big, big wagon. These wagons had sides you could pull up and down for when you need them. He was very strong. He took the whole side, of the big, big wagon, and he runs. He starts swinging at those *Rawhide* people. He chased the man who was driving the cattle two miles out of our village.[153]

Everybody was so frightened. Somebody ran to my mother: "Guleeg, run! Hagop is killing everybody!"

The Arabs could have stopped the cattle and let the women and children go to safety, and put the clothes away, but they did not care. They just walked over everybody.

My mother went to Hagop and saw him holding that big board and hitting everybody. My mother says, "What are you doing, Hagop?"

He cursed: "*Gashmi shaneem kooneem*! You sons of a bitch!"

The Arab boss came, "What's happening?" His people told him, and he said, "I'm going to go and kill that man." He took a big wooden club, a mallet, and he came: "Who did this! I want that man!" He wanted to challenge my father. My father had a poor friend, way over six feet tall. My father was not tall. My father used to help that man by giving him work. Sometimes you need two men to work, and he was a helper, and my father would feed him and give him money. My mother cooked and fed him. This man had a family, but he did not stay with them. He went there at night. This man was lazy. He did not want a steady job, and especially a lone job. So, my father was taking care of him.

When this Arab person came to challenge, my father said, "I did it."

The Arab said, "I'm going to challenge you."

This friend came and said, "No! You are not going to challenge him! You have to challenge me!"

This Arab saw what my short father did, and who knows what this tall man is going to do? He walked backward, "*La la la la la!*" He left. He goes with his people. He did not fight my father.

My father said later that he was kind of afraid because he was tired by then. But, my father saved the whole village.

A short while later, he returned to work in America. My grandmother came to live with us because my mother was young and alone, and beautiful. My mother had her own home, but my grandmother would cook for Mary and I and take care of us, while my mother was head of the house; she did the outside chores, and she would go work with her friends and cousins in their fields.[154] My mother would comb our hair in the morning and send us to school. I started school when I was four years old. The teachers used to give me raisins and teach me '*ayp, pen, keem,*' little alphabet, little song, then make me take a nap and wake me up. Mary went, too. I was very smart. I was head of my class.

Once my grandmother came to stay with us, she loved it. She never wanted to go back to her house. Every weekend, she used to take me to stay in her house. Mary stayed with my mother. Father had a lot of animals, but my grandmother had a lot of fields and had to hire animals to cultivate the fields. After Pa came from America, he did all those things.

It did not take too long before the War started, the massacres. The village crier comes and yells at you to give you news because we did not have any newspapers or magazines.

The crier yelled, "The war is starting. We don't know what is going to happen, but I want everybody to hear about the war to get ready."

Everybody started shaking and shivering. They knew the torturing was coming. They knew the horror was coming. In that state everybody lived.[155]

They started gathering all the young men to send to the war. All the men that could get away to America, they did. They would run away anywhere and hide. They did not stay in the village at all because the Turks would kill them. Whomever the Turks could hold onto, they took, the very young ones, about 20 or 22. They gathered all the young men to take in the Turkish army. Uncle Bedros was there. They took him. They took all the young men away. After the Turkish soldiers had gathered the young men to send to the war, they started with the older men, torturing some of them. In the *konagh*,[156] the house for torture and jail, the Turks put their feet in salt water and then starting whipping and whipping until the blood is running. The Turks could not get men like my father, so they picked on young men like Der Hovanessian.[157] They picked on the young men that were educated or that confronted them.

Even after that, the Turks were not satisfied. It did not take very long. The Turkish government stationed about 30 soldiers right in Tadem. The soldiers would be stationed there a few days and then go, and after a few days, the soldiers came back. They did it so systematic.

A few months, and the massacres started. The Turks started torturing, collecting people, questioning people. They question the people, and then let them go a week or two, and then take the villagers back. They started torture like a fire.

Every day, somebody knocks. The soldiers started knocking on the doors and asking for ammunition every day. People started hiding it, in the fields, underground, so they knew it was safe. They did not tell each other where. All of the village did that. Some of them had wells in their homes, so they hid things in the wells.

Papa had a sword, all colors, red on the bottom, then green, and silver on the top, hanging on the wall.[158] We did not want to give that sword. We did not have a well in our home. We went down the fields. My mother dug and hid it, so if we needed it, we would have it. Everybody tried to hide things in the fields, underground, anywhere it was safe. Papa had three guns. We had to keep the smallest one at home. We wanted to fight. If the Turks came for us, we could shoot them. But, the Turkish government did it so systematic. We had no power. We did not have any young men now. [159] Who is going to fight if the young men are not there? We did not have a group of men to fight. It was only old men and women left.[160]

The crier announced, "The government demands this, the government demands that. Do it if you want to save your life. Nothing will happen to you and your children if you do these things." People had to obey, but we'd had so much bad experience with the Turks, we began to look after ourselves. The Turks had never cared about the Armenian women, children, anybody. Every day they knocked and started asking for different things.

The priests started visiting the houses. "Please, no matter what they ask of you, let them have it, or they're going to torture you and they are going to take it away."

After they couldn't find any men because they had run away or were hiding or they had taken them for soldiering, the soldiers started asking for the women. They start asking for my mother. The Turks wanted to question my mother about my father. The Turks hated my father because, anything bad they had asked him, he never did it. We had, around the Tadem village, all the big Turkish men. They wanted to be the boss, the conquerors. Before, years ago, if you had a grown-up daughter, they would come and ask for the girl for the night, and you had to let her go for the night. But this had stopped years before the war when they asked my father and uncles.[161] The Turks could not come and demand their wives or women. My father said, "No. You can't do that to my women. You can't do that to my daughter." That's why they were so against him. The Turks always wanted to take something out of you. My father would confront them. They had all grown up like brothers in the village. My father knew the Turks' idea was always to take something out of you. To always take. To say, *do this!* and *do that!*

We wanted to live free. We wanted freedom. To be on our own. We did not want to live under dictators. They were like dictators in our little village. We did find our freedom,[162] but, when this war came, the Turks wanted to take advantage to do the same bad things—and they did.

My mother, every morning, went with the shepherds to the mountains, on her knees, so they wouldn't know there was a person going, so they couldn't get at her. She went in the morning and came in the night with the shepherds, to see us, to stay with us, and then go again the next morning. When the soldiers knocked on the door, they asked for the head of the house, which was my mother. We said, "We don't know. She's not home. We don't know where she is." They came inside and looked all through the house, in all the closets, they looked everywhere, but they could not find her. Then, the soldiers leave villagers alone a couple of weeks—and then the soldiers come again.

The town crier would come again and yell, "The government demands this. The government demands that. You should obey if you want to save your own life. Nothing is going to happen to you and your children if you obey."

We had to obey, but we had so much experience with the Turks, that everybody looked to themselves. You could not trust the Turkish government. Now look at—

[Pause. Eva states, "I have to tell you that after because I don't want it on the tape."]

…Everybody did what is the best for them. So, my mother went every morning to the mountains with the shepherds so no Turks could get at her.

After the Turkish government took all the ammunition and everything they saw, they decided you still have more. They started again to force the villagers to give everything they had.

The soldiers took the women they found to the *konagh*. They tortured them. No woman would talk about it, but you can imagine what they did to the women. If a woman was beautiful, they raped her and do everything. If they did not like her, they whipped her, feet, or body, or anything. They took her clothes and whipped her naked. Every kind of torture the Turks could think of to hurt you they did, to hurt you so you talk, you give secrets like this young man was doing something for this group or that group.[163]

Then the Turkish soldiers collected all the old men. They took them to a gorge, shot them, and those old men fell right down. The Turks took the young boys, like Hovannes, Krikor's brother, around twelve years old, and said they must transfer food for the government. We did not have trains or any transportation, so the Turks took the animals and young boys. In that group, they took about fifty from our village. They did the same in every village. Some of those boys came back, unhurt, but many of those young boys did not come back. I do not know if they died on the transfer or what happened.[164]

After that, the massacre time came.

The town crier came again yelling that they were going to take all of us away from our houses, but … they're not going to hurt any women: "Don't be afraid. Nobody is going to touch you. Only the government is going to change your places. You are going to leave your houses, and you are going to live in other cities."

They started moving us. They said, you are going to move around until the government commands where you are going to stay. They say, Don't worry. We are only doing the government's command. Everyone was forced a different way; everyone got lost that way; they died of hunger; the soldiers took them to Der-el-Zor, the desert. There is a song about Der-el-Zor.[165] You could be taken along the way, like I was taken in Mardin. Otherwise, you die of hunger. You run away if you have a chance. Everyone got lost that way. Each group the Turks took them different ways. The first group they took toward Malatia. You do not know what is going to happen. You go a certain place, and the Turks change the soldiers and hand you to those. Then those soldiers would go back to their stations. I was the last group that went.

In the middle of the collections, one group the Turks did not even take anywhere. My grandmother was in that group. Some crawled back half dead. Their necks were hanging, their hands and shoulders all cut. The blood was running down. My mother bandaged them. My mother nursed them.

After that, they collected twice more. They did it so systematic. The Turks did that gathering every other week, over and over again, until nobody was left—only those whom the *aghas* pick because they need workers in their houses. There were about 10 Turkish families in our village. Each had about three or four grown up children, as soldiers and all. They were strong. Now we did not have any ammunition, we did not have anything, but they wanted to move us away! They told us to sell our things if you can, but how much could we sell? But the Turks and Kurds came and robbed the houses and took our food and everything we had. Whoever could get there first, they grabbed everything the Armenian people had. My mother sold some of the things we had. She went to Mezre and sold some things. We had to buy a donkey to travel with. Whatever we could carry, we had to put it on the donkey.

We went to the first group for deportation. We had to sit at the end of the village near the brook where there was a square. At night we slept there to go the next day to move away. When morning came, one of the Turks came and threatened my mother that we were not going to go too far away because they were going to kill us, they did not want Hagop's family to live. He said, "Why don't you leave the children here with the group and come to our house? We can save you, but we can't save the children."[166]

My mother was thinking about that all night long. When morning came, she gave each of us…like a school bag…and she filled it with all the food she could from the items that we had brought. We had a donkey, and my mother had gotten food ready and all the clothes we could carry on that donkey. She said to my aunt, my father's sister,[167] "Overnight I made up my mind that I'm going to tell the children that little by little if they can escape this, to go and hide in those empty houses. If I can, I am, too. If I can't, or any of the children come here, you take care of them."

She told me, "We're not going to go. Now, Eva, you have to take Mary and Elizabeth and run away and hide somewhere—but do it systematically so the Turks won't suspect that you are going." Mary was older than me, but she was kind of shy and backward. But we had Elizabeth, four years old, and she was just like me.

My mother had given us each a bag, like a school bag, that she had put in all the food items. In back of our house, there was a bee house. One of our neighbors had bees. I put that bag over my shoulder, I held Elizabeth's hand,[168] and then we told Mary to go before us because we could go faster than Mary. We did not want to leave her there. If she was alone and we are gone, she might have stayed with my mother. So little by little … [Eva: "I will show you how … if the group is there, we go like this (Eva takes a tiny step, looking nonchalant) and we don't even look… I hold Elizabeth's hand, and we are going like this…."]. Sometimes we stopped and looked around so nobody would suspect we are running away. That way we went a quarter of a mile.

There was a house then, and it was up the hill. We started running. We ran where our mother told us, a certain corner, to that bee house that was back of our house. She said that if there was any food left or anything, next day we can gather and bring it. We got Mary there first. She was not sick or anything, but if we were with her, she could do better than if she was alone. I was the one who would go alone and find things.

We stayed there a few hours. We had gone early in the morning, about 7:00 o'clock, and about 9:00 or 10:00 o'clock, mother came. We all stayed there because it was a ragged place. The Turks or Kurds would not look there. There was not anything they were going to want to grab. The rags were hanging, and most people were afraid of the bees. We were afraid of the bee house. We had to tie our heads and put our hands inside our sleeves. The bees were not there, but one, two, or three would come once in a while, and we chased them away. We stayed there until it got dark.

After the darkness, mother said to go to a certain place where there was a family named Kulangants.[169] There is a lady married to a Turkish soldier. A lot of Turkish soldiers had come to take us away, kill the Armenians, and empty the village. The government had told them to do that. This woman, Guleeg, married one of those soldiers, but he was a very, very nice young man.

My mother said to tell Guleeg that we are saved, and what shall we do? Could she hide us if we come? Nobody knew we were alive. That group they took away toward Malatia. Everybody was gone, except the Turk people took some of them in their houses.

My grandmother and my aunt were still in the village, too. The day before, one of their Turkish friends took them to their house because Marnos had a lot of money. She had lots of money and jewelry. She had all gold. Marnos had not just gold but those big five gold pieces—we called it *behsheg-uleek*—and she had 25 pieces of those as a necklace.[170] This Turkish lady wanted it, and she is Turkish, so she can take. She said, "I'll hide you if you give me that."

Auntie Marnos said, "I'm going to bring my baby and my mother. If you send me to work in the fields, at least my mother can take care of my baby." The baby's name was Takouhi.

I went to this lady, Guleeg Karagulian. I went with Mary. Elizabeth was only four years old, the poor thing, and she stayed with mother. This lady took me in her arms and kissed me. She said, "Tell your mother to come. I'll hide her." She told us the Kulangants home is empty. In the barrels where they used to keep wheat and grain, we might to able to find a little flour or something. "You go there," she said, "and I'll bring you food."

Mary and I went, in the night, before the light was up, it was dark, and found mother. We all came to that empty Kulangants house, and next door opposite was this young woman. She had Armenians hidden. She was very pretty. She had married a Turkish soldier. There were a lot of soldiers there to take us away or to protect the village. They did not protect the village, but they killed the Armenians or emptied that village. The government had called them to do that, so the soldiers were stationed there. Guleeg married one of the Turkish soldiers, but he was a very, very nice young man.

We slept there. We rested. I was eight or nine years old then. Guleeg said she would help us, and if we were hungry, she would cook. She would tell her husband that we were great friends of hers, and we were. My father was friends of the son over here, in Malden, near Watertown (Massachusetts). Guleeg's husband never brought her here because he was so mad that she married a Turkish soldier, but he [the Turkish soldier] was a very nice man. So Guleeg died somewhere in the old country.

We stayed quite some time. We had to stay in the *marak*, like a cellar, where there was dry hay for the animals.

[Eva begins talking in Armenian with Rose. Rose suddenly exclaims, "Really! That's the place where she married the Turk!"]

That was where mother married that Turkish soldier. We never mentioned that while she was alive.

[Rose interrupts, "Papa never knew, did he?" Eva responds, "Oh, no, no. Papa would not understand that."]

… but he was a very nice man. Mother had to get married because the Turks came and took people again. Groups and groups they kept taking! This Turkish soldier was protecting us because my mother married him. After a week or two, he had some kind of sickness, and he died. He didn't live more than three weeks. He must have been sick before; there was lot of sickness in the wartime, like influenza. We were left alone again.

This time we went to my mother's niece, Yeva, who was in a different section of the village, in a Turkish house with her little Melkon. Somebody was protecting her.[171] Yeva did not get married, but she was living with him. The Turk's wife was there, but Turks can have more than one or two wives. So we went over to that section of the village, to the other end of the village. We were in the center, but my mother thought it was too much for Guleeg [Karagulian]. The Turks were suspecting her. They went to her house, and they inspected it to see if she was hiding people, so we lived at Yeva's a month or so. Then they came and took us again. They took us to Mezre.

Mother was hiding with Yeva.[172] Mary was down the mountains to graze the lambs. They took me and Elizabeth. Elizabeth was playing with the Turkish children. She had a white veil on and was dressed like them so they wouldn't know if she was Armenian or not. I was in that Turkish house, but the Turkish woman pushed us outside when the soldiers came. They grabbed me and took me to Mezre. They took many, many women, and they were all nice to me.

We were in a graveyard. All the soldiers had their swords around the group of people so they wouldn't run this way or that. There were brick walls anyway.[173]

I didn't know what to do. I saw a soldier dressed, all medals on him. He was sitting there, young and strong. "Gee," I said, "if ever I could get over there." I took Elizabeth's hand, and then I did the same thing, little by little, every one or two steps, every one or two steps, I went. From the other end to that end, I reached where he was. I started crying.

He asked me, "Why do you cry, my daughter?"

I said that my mother was behind, my mother was married to a Turkish soldier, and that the soldiers saw us and got hold of us, my little sister and me, and we don't have anybody here, we're between all strangers.

He said, "What village do you come from?"

They had gathered every village around Mezre, quite a few villages, Hussenig, Kesserig, Yegheki, and Soursouri. They put the Armenians in that cemetery. It wasn't just our village.

I said, "Tadem."

He called, "Is there anybody here from Tadem?"

There was one old Turkish man nearby.

The soldier said, "Do you know these two little girls?"

The man said yes.

He said, "Do you know their mother?" The man said yes.

The soldier said, "I want you to take care of them and take them and hand them to their mother. If you don't, you have to answer to me." Then he put his hand in his pocket, took all the change he could in his hand, and gave it to me. "You take this, so if you're hungry or anything, you can buy something and eat."

[Pause. Eva starts crying.]

..so he asked that man to take us to my mother. My aunt was in Yegheki working for the Turkish government. She was working to take the flour, the wheat, to grind and bring to the soldiers to eat. She used to pass by the road.

It took about an hour to walk back to Tadem, so I told this man to leave me. I told this old Turkish man, "I don't want to go to Tadem."

He said, "Where do you want to go?"

I said, "My aunt will pass here in a little while. If you leave me here, she will find me."

He said, "I have to stay with you until she comes and takes you."

He stayed a long time, and my Aunt did not come. He said, "I have to go." So, he went to Tadem and told my mother that I was waiting for my aunt with my sister, and I'm going to go to my Aunt's house. My mother had that news.

A little later, my aunt came and took me and Elizabeth to her house in Yegheki. My mother came. We couldn't stay there because my aunt could not feed us. We walked to the village where my mother worked in the fields.

She will work the lands if they don't take us again. At the harvest time, there was a lot of grain and everything. It was fall. So, we went to Tadem.

We changed our place. We went to the place of Anna, Bedros' wife, who lived in another section of the village. This Turkish woman[174] was saving Anna. She used to sleep there, eat there, and work there.

We lived there for a while, but nobody was taking care of us. My mother was independent. She goes into the fields. It was fall now. My mother looked in the ground after the harvest, for what was left, and collected it. There was a lot on the ground from the crop. My mother got a whole bagful.[175]

We hid in the *marak* next door. No homes, nothing; we were homeless. My mother worked in the fields because there was a lot of grain.

Meanwhile she told us there were a lot of chickens running around the houses and I should go and catch and bring them so we could eat. Mary would come with me and Elizabeth. If I caught any, I gave them to Mary to hold. Elizabeth would be somewhere near us because she couldn't stay with mother or go with mother.

We hide in the *maraks*. Nobody bothers us for a while. Sometimes they come and gather you all and take you in a group, but after that group has gone, you're on your own again. No home. Nothing. You don't know where you are going to live. Some corner or something—just like the homeless now. We were homeless. So, we lived in those *maraks* where Anna lived, her house. We stayed in her house or her uncle's house because there were doors between them. We open the doors and go back and forth.

So that is where the Effendi, who knew who I was, spied me. When he came, I ran.

He chased me and said, "You have to tell me where your mother is."

I said, "Everyone's dead! I don't know where my mother is! I don't know anybody! I have only my little sister."

We lived there, in that condition, about two or three months.

[Pause.... Rose speaks encouraging words in Armenian to Eva.]

This story is full in me, all in my body. My mother had to always hide. I was the man of the house—at that age—the provider. I was eight, not quite nine. I had to take care of my sisters. I always was bright and very smart. I don't want to praise myself, but mother was depending on me because anything she couldn't do, she would ask me to do for her. That was where we caught chickens, day after day, and we ate them.

The climate started to cool. It was fall.

My mother said, "We can't do this. I'll go down to Mezre and see if Father has sent us any money or anything to the American Consul."[176] We wanted to see if we got any money or anything because the Turks took all of our money and all.

Once in a while, we saw Auntie Marnos. She didn't have any money now either. She couldn't help us any.

My mother said, "We have to change our place and go live near my other sister Takouhi in Yegheki."

After we came there, we hired a house. Marnos came.

My grandmother was killed by then. My grandmother had been with my Aunt Marnos, who was so rich. The khanum had taken her in because Marnos had all that money. After she got the money, the khanum was satisfied; she drove my grandmother out: "We don't want her anymore. We're under pressure from the government. The only thing I'll do is save you and your baby if you want to stay. If you don't want to stay, you go, too." I don't think my grandmother was more than sixty.

That night my Aunt Marnos went and hid somewhere the Turkish woman didn't know; she didn't trust her. Aunt Marnos left her baby there and hid that night, but she did not tell that Turkish woman where. After the night passed, then Marnos came out. That is the way our life was. That's what mother did. That's what everyone did. They hide and they didn't tell anyone where. My mother, Yeva, and another woman had to go hide in the outside, in the outhouse, in all that stink. Those three women used to go and hide under that filth and smell for about twelve hours before they could come out, and then my mother would be free and come and find us.

The Turks took my grandmother in a group, to a nearby Turkish village, and there they just killed the Armenians with stones and knives and all.[177] The soldiers called the wild men, the wild women, and wild children from a nearby Turkish village: "Come on. Help us kill this enemy." The wild Turkish women and children and men, young and old, came with stones and big sticks and helped the soldiers to kill most of the Armenians in that convoy. The soldiers killed most of them, and the ones they didn't kill, the Turks helped killed by stones and all.

The Turks had taken their clothes; they had taken everything they had. Some women were alive, and they crawled back the next day, with their necks hanging down, half slit. They came to one house that was near where we lived. Mother was nursing them and feeding them like a nurse. She bandaged their wounds.[178] She put together the neck and tied it up. One of mother's cousins had married a Turkish lieutenant—mother had a lot of cousins—and they lived right near us. This cousin used to bring to those that were half killed and half alive—some of them died and some of them stayed alive—all the food and clothes that she could get. Then her husband called her and told her she shouldn't do that because he could lose his job.

After a while, we had to move on because they were after mother. They wanted to find her and kill her. We went from one place to another. So we went to Aunt Takouhi's village and hired a house that was empty because they took the Armenians away. They had done the same thing in that village. Everybody else is not alive. Only some of the Armenians were alive who had the best Turkish friends or had married Turks.

We stayed there no more than two weeks with Aunt Marnos and her baby. Mother went always where Charlie's wife Azni was, her mother and father's home. Her father was the governor's ... not wagoneer ...but chauffeur. He would take the governor to government houses every morning and bring him back. That was his job.[179] My mother used to visit them a lot, and all day long she would stay there because it was safer. The first time I was taken to the graveyard [in Mezre], she was there, safe, she was very near me, but she did not come out because she thought we were young, and nothing would happen to us.

This time when mother went, the Turks came to gather up the Yeghekitzi. The Turks came to gather again. They knocked on the door and yelled, "You have to come out." They came and pushed you away if you're hiding. We were in the fields, hiding under the big pile of hay. The Turks looked through everything. They put their swords into that to find us. They hit one of us and gathered us. They put us the same way in Mezre. My mother did not come and ask for us. She was hiding somewhere in Yegheki. So, the Turks took us away. Mother may have been in the same house because over there the Turkish soldiers never went and looked around because Azni's father was working for the governor, the *Vali*.[180]

This was the last collection. I had saved myself from two collections. This time, I did not try. I said to myself, "How long can I do that? I will just go."

There were so many people, hundreds and hundreds of people, when we started walking. Every stop, we tried to leave Elizabeth at the nearest village, so mother would come next day and find her. But, no, Elizabeth would cry and yell, "Mother! Eva! Mother! Eva!" She would cry and find us. We tried so hard to lose her, so she won't be far away from home. It would be easy for mother to come and find her, and we couldn't keep her. We had been walking about five days. We were near our home yet. One day, when we sat to rest at night, with all the group of the people, hundreds and hundreds, we went and stood in line for a piece of bread. The soldiers count how many you are, and they give you one loaf and one half, or one loaf, or half a loaf. They ration it out as the people are.

We knew Elizabeth was hungry. She was so young and all. When we sat down, we hid and then went in the back of her and threw a piece of bread in front of her, so she could take it and eat it. We did that for two or three days, and finally we didn't find her anymore. We were five or six villages away, like Auburn or Leicester,[181] before we lost her. It is like when you go to New York [from Worcester], how many little towns there are. I couldn't measure because I was young, and I wouldn't know.

Until now we don't know what happened to her. But she was crying and yelling every minute of every day: "I want my sisters. Where are you, Eva? Where are you, Mary? I want my sisters." I still hear her voice. It burns my heart. We didn't know if she got killed, or if somebody took her for adoption or anything[182] Until now we do not know.

Elizabeth was following the crowd, and we wanted to lose her. We did not hold her or take her. Our intention was good, but I am sorry we did that now. Maybe if we had taken her with us, somewhere, she would have been alive now. I don't know. But we wanted to leave her near our town so my mother could find her, so we lost her. We didn't see her anymore. *[Eva to her younger sister Rose:]* She looked just like you.

[Long pause]

After that, we went further and further. I had hunger for my mother, my family.

We went way deep, deep in the Turkish land.[183] Every night we slept in the fields. If the Turkish soldiers wanted to kill somebody, they killed them.

They took all the young girls; every night they used[184] the young girls, and in the morning, they let them go. All the way that they went to Arabia they did that.[185]

The Çetes[186] start doing so many dirty things. They did all the dirty things they could do. If a woman was pregnant, they would open her with the sword, take that baby on the sword, and twirl it.[187] That is how bad they were.

[pause]

And now the Turks claim they never did such a thing. But I saw it with my own eyes, in my young days, my childhood, they did all those things…."

One night after we got up, in a village way down near Arabia, my Aunt said, "I can't carry the baby anymore. I'm going to leave her. This is a village. Maybe somebody will come and take her away." We left her at a door and walked away.[188] *[pause]* She couldn't take care of us. We took care of us.

We walked another two or three days, deeper to Arabia, past Dikranogerd, near Mardin. Dikranogerd was where the Armenian king lived, and there was a lake there, Lake Moura, we called it. When we arrived there, all the Turkish people would come and pick the young people and Armenian girls.

About twenty days we had been walking. I was nine years old. The thirst. The hunger. They gave us a little piece of bread.

Yohaper was there. She was there but did not come near us.[189] Vartanoush Avlav, one of our cousins, tried to help us a few times. She found some shoes and gave them to us. We had been barefoot. Vartanous Avlav was one of our cousins (she lived in Watertown [Massachusetts]). Blood was running from our feet, all sores. In Dikranogerd, they took eighteen or twenty Armenians to the hospital to be nursing, to work for the soldiers. I was too young to do that. Yohaper went there. Vartanoush Avlav went there. So now only the younger people and older people were left.

Aunt Marnos had worn two dresses, one of top of the other. The nice clothes underneath were all pleated and white. Aunt Marnos had on pants called *shalvars*. The nice clothes were in the *shalvars*. Every night when we went by a village, she tore a part of her nice dress. She cut one nice piece of white cloth—material for ladies—and we went and exchanged it for food with ladies.[190] We did not have any money. The women had food, but they wanted us to give them something before they gave us any food. The Turkish soldiers would give us a little piece of bread, a ration.

When we came to this little village, Aunt Marnos sent me for food. She did not go. She used to send me.[191] When she sent me, somebody saw me and came and told the soldiers that they wanted me. They told the soldiers, "We want that girl." When they came to take me, I hid. But Mary and I used to dress the same. They saw Mary and thought she was me.

Mary said, "I can't walk any more. I have to go." I made it short, but it was a long, long way to go. Day after day…. so Mary went.

We walked. Hunger. No drinks. We drank rainwater if it was in little places. We bent down and drank. There wasn't much sun. It wasn't too hot because it was fall.

There weren't many people now. Some people went. Some people were killed on the way. Some fell sick and couldn't walk anymore. The soldiers left them there for the local Turks to kill them, so they get rid of them. There was a little group left. It was all the way, from our country to Mardin, bodies. Bones and bodies, we had to walk over them.[192]

Two days after Mary went, someone came on a horse. They are Chechen. Like Russian people, they had all bullets on their chest and a long uniform. One had been sent to look for a nice little girl. He saw me. There weren't hundreds and hundreds of people anymore. There was a little group left. Everybody was going somewhere.

I had to go somewhere because Auntie told me every day that she doesn't want to take care of us. If we are not with her, she might go with somebody, too, to save herself.

I said, "Okay, Aunt Marnos, if you want me, too. Mary went anyway." In my mind, I want to be near Mary. Someday we might meet each other. She was one or two villages away. Someday we might get together.

The man put me back of him on the horse and took me from the hills that was Mardin. I did not know where it was then. There was another little girl in our small group. She was young but tall. This man took her, too. I never saw her afterward. He put me on the horse with him, and she walked with us. We went to Mardin.

I never saw Auntie Marnos again.

In Mardin, I saw the German officers and the Germans, who were helping the Turks. German soldiers were working there. Before now, it was all Turkish soldiers. The Germans were the brains of the deportations. The

Germans told the Turkish government how to get rid of us because we wanted freedom. The Germans had told the Turkish government, "The more the Armenians stay, the more they will be more, and the more they will demand. You'd better control them while you have the chance to."[193]

The man on horseback took me into a Syrian home. I was so hungry. They brought an Armenian person and spoke to me through her. They asked me who was alive, who was I, who was my family.

I said, "My father and uncle are in America. My mother is left back in the old country. My aunt was with me, but I have left her now. She is still in the group. This man asked for a nice girl. I don't know where he is going to take me."

They said, "Where this man is going to take you is a very nice home, but when you go there, don't tell them that your father or your uncle are alive, and they are in America. Say everybody is dead. Don't say your mother is alive and back in the country. Tell them that they're all dead."

So that's what I did.

A little girl came. She's not little, but she is like a midget. I thought she was a girl, but afterwards they told me she was about 20 or something. She was holding my hand. She wants to talk to me. *[Eva to her young sister Rose: "Come over here and hold my hand, so I can show you." Rose becomes flustered; she rises, they lock hands, and Rose breaks into a nervous but excited grin as she is finally invited to be a part of the family history. Eva pulls Rose, "Gel! Gel! Get! Get!" Rose exclaims, "What is 'gel! gel!' Eva explains that is the Turkish for "Come, come! Come, come! Come, come!"]*

She pulls me! She is holding me the way I am holding on you! "*Gel! Gel! Get! Get!*"

She took me to this nice, big house. There were two ladies waiting, and they talked to each other, and of course I don't understand. They don't know Turkish or other languages. Right away they put me in a tub of hot water; they washed me, they combed my hair, they dressed me up, and said, "Nice! Nice!" I had some bugs in my hair by then. All the refugees were dirty and had bugs in their hair. The lady goes to different houses to work; she washed the people and washed their hair because they had picked up bugs in their hair. She dressed them up. Others called her special for this. This *"Gel! Gel! Get! Get!"* woman was there with her whole family in one section of the house. They live there and they work for my adoptive mother. They used to take us to the bathhouse, carry our things. My adoptive mother didn't work except to cook a little for her husband. The others did the other work, but she wouldn't let others do that because her husband wouldn't eat it or wanted it cleaner. So, they did not have a cook.

I slept there at night, nice and clean. I was so hungry! They fed me pilaf with *shereh*! I thought the pilaf was all meat. I didn't know it was *shereh*. I had never seen it. In our country, we just had bulghur. We did not have *shereh*, all fried and the pilaf cooked with it. It was delicious. I slept that night, nice and clean.

The next day, I woke up and they were all there. All the neighbors and cousins came to see me. My adoptive mother's sister came, who was married and had children. Her brother, who had a high job in the government, and his wife came. They were the governing body of Mardin. He was not a governor, but he had a high job in the government. He came and saw me. They introduced me all that week. They liked me.

So, I lived. My adoptive mother was a very kind woman. They had to call her honorable terms, like "Highness" or "Honor." My adoptive father was just in the government. He was Effendi.[194] My adoptive mother was good, but very homely. She had a fat, long face, and she had pockmarks.[195] She and my adoptive father were cousins. His first wife died, and he had three boys. My adoptive mother, she must have been an old maid, and she married him to take care of the boys, to make a home and wife for him. But she wanted a little girl. My adoptive mother didn't have any children.

I stayed in that house three years. She took very good care of me. They bought me nice clothes. They had the oldest son's daughter with them, and she was very, very jealous. She always used to hit me and try to find faults with me.[196] My mother would tell her, "Don't do that." My mother loved her, too, but she knew that someday she was going to go to her father. My mother put in right away for adoption of me, and she gave me a name. She said, "If I die, everything will go to her." Her name was Baheyah *khanum*. I was Shofkeeah.[197] That other girl was Fatmah. The three sons were Bahauddin, Jalal, and Jarad. My father's name was Hassan *effendi mootwali*. He was "mootwali" because he belonged to that religion.

My mother took very good care of me. She started teaching me Arabic. She used to hold any item in her hand, and tell me three times: *muher*, salt. And she'd say, "Mmmmmm," with her finger up. That means, "If you forget, you're going to get a lickin'." So, I had to remember *muher*. Or she'd tell me, *khubus*, bread, and "Mmmmm!" In three months, I captured Arabic, not because I was smart but because she knew how to teach, or I was frightened not to learn. She would hold a glass of water, and she would tell me, *maa*. She taught me good Arabic. Some girls had been there two years or two years and a half before me, but they could not talk Arabic as good as me. Their families knew Turkish. Some of them knew Turkish, and it was easier for them because they knew some words anyway, so they did not learn quicker, right away as I did. My mother was a good teacher, knowledgeable because of her class. She knew what to do. She came from a big family background. She didn't know how to write or read, but she had brains. She taught me all she knew. I did not learn all her cooking because I didn't cook, I was young, but some I remember now and do it.

One day, some beggar was knocking downstairs to ask for food. I went to open the door, and I knew one of the ladies. I said, "Mariam *Bajii*, *vos eench gunes*? What are you doing here?"

She said in Turkish, "Who are you?" She talks Turkish.

I said, "*Yes nundugents Takouhi karooteenem.*" I am Takouhi's sister daughter from Tadem."

Then I didn't talk any more. No matter what question she asked me, how old are you?, what are you doing here?, I didn't answer because she was right next door—like a twin home—to my Aunt Takouhi in Yegheki, and my mother will be with my Aunt, and if Mariam *Bajii* goes, she will tell them. I told her who I was, so she'd know, but I didn't talk after that. I was walking, and they were coming to beg, to get food and something, and they are coming after me. They talked, but I still didn't answer, no matter what they said. They came upstairs.

The woman with Mariam *Bajii* knew a little Arabic. She said, "We know this girl. We know her mother and the family."

My mother asked me, "Do you know them?"

I said, "Oh, no. I never saw them. I never knew them." Because my adoptive mother had told me, "I never want you to talk Armenian or to say you're Armenian. You're going to be my daughter. I'm going to adopt you, and you're going to be my daughter." You know, they didn't all adopt the orphans. They just make the orphans work. But my adoptive mother was good enough to do that. She took good care of me. I didn't want to be against her. I liked her as much as my mother.[198] When my mother came, I didn't want her.

Those women went back to Kharpert and told my mother I was alive. Kharpert was far, far away, with so many villages and towns before you could come to Mardin. One of my mother's cousins was in Mardin. She must have been married with an Arab or something. She came after me. She found out where I was. She asked, and those ladies must have given the direction of the house where I lived. She came after me to talk to me. *Hazervat* her name was. Her grandmother and my grandmother were first cousins.

She said, "I'm going back home. I want to take you. You come with me."

I said, "Oh, no. I'm going to stay with my adoptive mother here. I like my mother, and I'm going to stay here." I refused.

In three days, she came back again and did the same thing, but I would not go. She went back to Kharpert and told my mother where I was, what house I was, and how it was. So, I leave this here....

One morning I went downtown. My mother used to send me to buy little things. Sometimes the workers forget to buy little things. We had about twenty stores that belonged to my father. He owned their big mosque, too. His ancestors made it and gave it to the city of Mardin. He used to collect money from his stores and spend it on their mosque. They get up and yell "*Allah!....*"

I had some roasted chickpeas and raisins in my pocket. This beggar girl was looking on the ground, all over, to find some food, to eat. She didn't look up. She just look on the ground and in the corners to find something to eat.[199] My sister! She was all brown. The color of wood.

I looked at her, and I looked. I went. I didn't talk. I went three times and gave her some raisins and chickpeas. And I turn back to go. But I couldn't go. Seems to me, they chained my leg. I couldn't go away. I came back again and gave food to her. Then I wanted to go, but I couldn't go. Again, I feel chained. I turned around and said, "Who are you?" in Turkish.

She said, "I'm a Kurd."

I said, "I'm Eva. Aren't you Mary?"

Oh, she started crying and crying! She hugged me, and I hugged her. She said, "Yes, yes, yes, I'm Mary." She was speaking Kurdish. I understood that language. I was talking five languages, but my mother turned me into *dhimmi*.[200] She should have backed me up to not forget those languages, but she used to tell me, "If you ever...." I will tell you that after the Aleppo part. Now we are with Mary....

I held her hand[201]—the way you hold my hand—and I took her to my house. The same lady they called to wash Mary up and dress her up in my clothes. I had so many we could share them. That lady lived down below, and she comes. Sometimes my mother calls a different lady to do better work. Those others were like gypsies. They had a whole house because they need them. Mary stayed with me, but she was very, very sickly. My adoptive mother said she was sickly, but Mary had never been sick back home, in our country. Mary was sick here. She was all burned, hungry, dried up inside her. There was a depression, and they had let her go. There was hunger in Syria. They couldn't keep her. They couldn't feed her. You could not find food. They told her to go, she's free to go, so she didn't stay in the villages. What is she going to do in the villages? She walked to the city to try to find anything to eat.[202] [203]

My adoptive parents kept her for three months. Then summer came. Every summer we went in a different direction for a vacation. They didn't want to take Mary because she was sick. They said, "We'll put her in an orphanage." They put her in the orphanage a month before we went, more than that maybe. I used to take her food and go see her every week and talk to her. She wanted lots of garlic and bread. In the old country, everybody used a lot of garlic. They put it on bread like peanut butter. They open up the garlic, peel it, and rub it on the bread. I took her two or three big garlics. I took her raisins and roasted chickpeas, dried food that would last. I took her a lot of other food, but she asked most for that. They gave her bread, rationing, in that orphanage, or the food, it isn't like here where they give food in a dish. Whatever I had. Dried figs. I used to take her a lot of cheese, Armenian cheese is in Arabia, too.

We went for vacation to Museybin and stayed about a month and a half, or more. Nobody was in school or anything, so you can have all summer. When we came back, I went to see her. She had passed away.[204] [205]

Six months after, mother came and found me. When she came, she had such a hard time, an awful, hard time. She wanted me so badly to go right away with her. She stayed in the Red Cross buildings. They had special places for the homeless Armenians, no other nationality. She wanted to take me there, but I wouldn't go.

So she said, "Then I'm going to stay here."

I told my mother and father that my mother wants to take me, but I don't want to go, and my mother doesn't have a place here (I didn't tell them that she had a place) and where is she going to stay? They said, "Let her stay here."

They were so nice and kind to her, but she was so mean and hateful to them though you couldn't blame her because all they did to us, and my mother sees them, that *they* did it. She never appreciated the kindness, all the gold, all the jewelry I had on my arms.

I even had gold bracelets on my feet. When I used to walk, the bells would ring.

My mother saw all this, but she didn't care. She wasn't nice to them at all. If she was a politician, she would have done differently, but she had so much the love of her country and her people. I don't blame her for that. I might have done the same. I am glad my father was not there. I think if they had killed my father, I think night and day my mother would have tried to kill them.

This family started ... they didn't want her there. They wanted to push her out. But they knew if they did that. I might just leave them and go with my mother. I would never back my mother up, but they knew I was very smart, so they were very gentle with her, but in conflict. Sometimes they used to tell me stories about "her kind." They said, "There was an Armenian woman who wanted to kill our king. She did herself up in a costume, and she went to work in the Turkish bathhouse." (*Eva states in an aside:* The people did not have a bath in their homes. They go to a bathhouse.) My mother said, "When our king went to have a bath there, she killed him. This Armenian lady killed our king." Her name was "Shavayee Adadavayee." They named my mother "Shavayee Adadavayee." My adoptive mother said, "She might some night kill us." My adoptive mother was suspicious of her that way.

I told my mother, "Why don't you be a little kinder with them. You are living here and all."

My mother said, "We don't have to live there. You come with me, and we can go live somewhere else. We don't need this!"

Every day my mother would get up in the morning and go the villages and look for Armenians. Another lady lived in the Red Cross, and every morning, she and my mother would meet each other and go from Mardin to those villages and look for those Armenians. My mother brought lots and lots of Armenians and put them into the Red Cross houses. They took them away from the Turkish houses.

My mother would tell them, "The Armenians are on their feet. Everybody would love to have you. They are going to help us." She talks to them, she brainwashes them, so they leave their husbands and their children to come. That is what my mother did in Mardin. She was a wonderful, wonderful person as an Armenian.

I decided now. I know they don't want her here, and I didn't know what to do, and then I decided. I told her, "Why don't you go and live in the Red Cross houses?"

She said, "No. I am not going to unless you come."

"I can't come. I'm not going to come with you." I said, "I'm not going back to the old country with you." If I had gone with her, she would have gone back to the country. She wouldn't have gone to Aleppo. I don't want to go. I said, "I don't want to be the way I was there. Without mother. Without father. You always hide. I don't tell this in front of them. You just leave us alone. Look at my sister Elizabeth I lost. It burns my heart! Mary died. You didn't come on time. I don't want to be that again. Now you would blame me, but I have told you."

My mother finally went to the Red Cross and would come visit me a couple of days a week. I felt sorry for her. I felt sorry for myself.

But the people used to talk about "that girl," me, you know, "her" family, "her" background, "her" this and that. Once in a while, when my mother got mad at me, she called me, "*Ajee!*" *Ajee* means *vorb*—orphan. I did not like that word. If she's adopted me, if I'm her daughter, she should call me, "*Charageegee!*" (Naughty girl!). She did not say that. She said, "*Gavour khazee!*" (Infidel's daughter!) or "*Kafir khazee!*" (Enemy's daughter!). She did not say it very often, but she did say it once in a while.

I figured, as young as I was, my mother would never call me that. Why am I staying there? When my mother's here, and I love my father?

there. That is where my mother married that boy and that lady, Yesabet [Elizabeth], who visited us from California. [Eva to her younger sister, Rose] You remember a few years ago? Do you remember them? Yesabet visited us with her little boy, her grandchild. She used to send us all those packages.[210] They came and stayed with us a week and a half. [Eva returns to narrative]. Well, mother married them, and we stayed all together until they went to Cilicia, to come to America from there. All those groups that came from Russia went there. Bedros came from Russia to Cilicia.[211] But of course that is not our story. We stayed in Aleppo.

We went to the American Consul for money my father sent us. Before my father sends us money, the American Consul gave us money because mother used to work, to go and break stones for the road, for about four weeks. My mother first sold my jewelry, and we lived on that. I think she did that purposefully so that I would not have them anymore. The jewelry was Arabic. If we had brought the jewelry to America, we would have had much more money because the jewelry was valuable. I had gold necklaces, brace-lets, and anklets. I had silver braided in my hair. They loved me, I think....

All the Armenian people had to live that way. There was no money. There was Depression in every city and town. There was hunger in every city. But the government was good, and all Armenian groups, like Dashnak, Red Cross, and the Armenian charities in America sent help. Some people like Agnes and them went and stood in line for soup. But we didn't go for soup. My mother wouldn't do that. My mother was an independent woman.

When Father started helping us, mother secured our passports. We came to Beirut and stayed not more than two weeks. There were such beau-tiful oranges! Beirut was such a pretty city. All oranges! Every home had its own tree and oranges! We stayed there a couple of weeks until my father secured our passports.

It was the first time I saw a banana! I had a penny. I went to the man and asked for banana. "What is that? I want to eat it." I knew what oranges were because my father used to go to Cilicia in the summers and bring us big, big oranges. But bananas I had never seen. I had pennies, so I went to the man selling bananas.

He said, "I can't give you a banana for that!" But, he did take the penny, and he gave me a banana.

Then we came to France. We stayed about two or three months. We had a cousin there who died. He was my mother's sister-in-law's brother. He was very agitated. In Italy, he was going to be a priest, but he couldn't and came to France. He took very good care of us. He took us everywhere. He helped us with our passports because an agent does that, and this man was a friend of the agent.

We came to America, to my father.

The marriages of Guleeg and her sisters—Marnos, Takouhi, Khatun, and Jooar—after the 1895 Great Massacres when their father was killed and their fate after the 1915 Genocide when her sisters' husbands were killed:

After 1895 Great Massacres

My mother's father had quarries and ten oxen. He was a stone maker and transporter. He had many workers. He had clay pots filled with gold pieces hidden in the storage kitchen. When the killing began [1895 Great Massacres], the Turks spent hours taking the clay pots of gold hidden in the pantry. All the wealth went. The wild and hungry Kurds came from the mountains, robbed the village, killed the people, and cleaned out the village in three hours. I don't know how my grandmother was saved. All the girls ran away, or somebody saved them.

The Armenians were hungry then, and my aunts married to different places because no one could take care of them anymore. My aunts were young and beautiful girls and came from a family with a good name, so others thought they would be good wives for their young men. So, Marnos got married in Sursuri village. Takouhi got married in Yegheki village. Khatun married a big family near Tadem. Jooar married into another big family, Bohajian. The girls got married right away because they were afraid like me and thought if they have to go through killings like this, they wanted a husband who could protect them. But my mother was very young, and she was the only one left. After a little while, a few weeks, people started to gather together and build up again, to be family and all.

My father Hagop was poor then, and he needed a job, so the Toomasians hired him to work for them. My father fell in love with mother, and mother did not like him. She never liked him! My father finally left that job, but he didn't leave her. Everywhere, every corner she went, he was there and said, "You are going to marry me. Don't forget. No one can come near you." He took his knife and showed it to her and said, "I will kill you if you don't marry me." She couldn't get rid of him, so she married him.

Note: The "courtship" of Hagop Haroian and Guleeg Toomasian reveals the devastation of the village, including the elimination of its patriarchal leadership. Had either Guleeg's father or Hagop's father been alive, the "courtship" would have been highly different. The village had a limited number of young men without fathers and with deep trauma. After the Great Massacres, many of men who had survived by hiding or other means went to America or Russia. In tragic irony, the Haroians had been one of the founding families (*yerli*) and main and wealthy clans of Tadem. When the Europeans had pushed for reform in the 1870s, the Sultan had appointed administrators for the villages in the interior, not a few of whom excelled in oppressing the Armenians and carrying out the massacres. Hagop Haroian's grandfather was targeted early by the village *agha*, Hadji Bego, who persecuted the Haroian patriarch—Ovanes Haroian—and stole all his lands. Ovanes Haroian's two strong teenage grandsons—Hagop and Poghos—then had to work the lands stolen by the *agha* to survive and feed their families. The result was that Hagop and Poghos were of the few young men spared during the Great Massacres due to the *agha*'s dependency on them.

After 1915 Genocide:

Takouhi: Takouhi wrote to us when she was in the old country. Takouhi got to France because my father helped her. They all came. They did not stay in the old country. They used to come to Aleppo and then to France. My father helped all of my mother's sisters. Every month, or every few months, he used to send about 25 dollars, and American money was big over there, so they lived on my father. After years, my mother's cousin Simo, who was also a friend of my father's because they worked together, started corresponding with my mother after we came to America. So, my mother said, "Why don't you go marry my sister Takouhi? So he went to France, and he got married, but he never came back here. They lived in France. Takouhi had been married in Yegheki, but she never had children. First, she went to Aleppo, and from there to France, and we used to correspond. My father would send her money. My father was a very kind, very good man. Do you remember little Sahag who came to work on our farm? Sahag married Vardanush's sister, Yessa, and my father and mother fixed that up.

Marnos: I never saw Marnos after I was apart from her. Someone said that something came up, and Marnos ran and hid, and she was choked in an Arabic *marak*. She hid herself under those hays and she was choked.[212] It may have been her, or someone else. I don't know as I never saw or heard from Marnos after I was separated from her. We never saw her baby Takouhi that we left at the door in the village square where we were sitting overnight.

Jooar: Jooar was Yeva's mother.

Khatun: I did not talk about Khatun because she was alive, but she wasn't with us. She was in another village with her own family. She was nearby Tadem, and her family was richer than ours was. Some Turks were friends of her family, so they took most of the things Khatun's family had. The Turks moved into their house and took everything that they want. The Turks took their animals, the horses, the cows, all the sheep, and they said, "So we'll save you." I think they did. That's the life we went through. After the Genocide, Khatun's daughter Yohaper came to America, so Yohaper used to help her mother. My father had sent Khatun money all the time. Khatun stayed in Aleppo. Yohaper was here, but she couldn't bring her.

Concluding Statement

…. That is the life we went through. That's the life I want to tell you about in Tadem. Tadem was a group, an Armenian community, and that is where I was born. I am Eva Hightaian. I am married now. I was Haroian before. I remember my young days.

Elaboration on Quote from *The Thirty-Year Genocide: Turkey's Destruction of Its Christian Minorities: 1894-1924*. Benny Morris and Dror Ze'evi. Cambridge: Harvard UP, 2019:

"The Christians of Turkey suffered three decades of persecution even though there were years of relative "quiet" between each murderous bout. This meant that the Armenians—less so the Greeks and Assyrians—underwent an almost unrelenting torment: an Armenian woman from eastern Anatolia, born in the 1880s, would likely have seen her parents killed in 1895…

…and she would have seen her uncle murdered, flayed, and burned, and her grandmother brutalized and murdered

… and her husband and son massacred in 1915…

…and she would have been gang raped, and she would have seen her mother's throat slit, and she would have seen her three children deported, one four-year-old daughter to disappear forever; one eleven-year old daughter to be transferred to a Muslim household, abused, abandoned, and dead; and one nine-year old daughter to be transferred to a Muslim household where she was slapped, humiliated with tattoos, called names ("Infidel's orphan!"), and indoctrinated into Islam….

… If she survived, she probably would have been raped and murdered in 1919-1924. Certainly, she would have been deported in that last genocidal phase." (page 502)

G<small>ULEEG</small> T<small>OOMASIAN</small> H<small>AROIAN</small>

The Rosetta Stone: Cannibalistic Language of Genocide Survivors —
Gil Harootunian, PhD, Editor

The value of having oral histories in the survivors' own language includes being able to study that language. For example, examining the survivors' language reveals they use the language of cannibalism, both literally and metaphorically, for the Genocide. My grandmother and others use the word "eat" to describe the Genocide. The Danish missionary, Maria Jacobsen, relates an instance of cannibalism of Armenian orphans: "22 July [1918]. We had a sudden visit from Lt. Gerber and Dr. Weng, who were to leave again next morning, taking Count Lütticau with them. They had lunch with Karen Marie and their evening meal with me. Lt. Gerber told us that there was a man and a woman in Mosul who had slaughtered 50 children and sold their cooked flesh on the market, and if the Germans had not strongly demanded that an investigation be undertaken, the government would not have done it. The result was that the man and woman were hanged" (2001, page 217). A missionary on-site during the 1894-1896 Great Massacres also notes cannibalism: "…most of the leading Protestants were slaughtered, and the flesh of their chief men carried round the market for sale at 10 paras (about 1d.) the oke…![213] (I may say that I thought this last piece of atrocity must be apocryphal, but we have heard it from four different quarters)" (Harris, 1897, page 168).[214]

"Eating" the Armenians took different forms. Balakian writes the hungry dogs, jackals, foxes, and wolves would "eat the lives ones first" especially weakened children unable to fend them off (Balakian, Grigoris, 2009, page 225, 250). The testimony of survivors, witnesses, and perpetrators bear out this theme repeatedly, for both the Great Massacres and the Genocide. During the Great Massacres, Northrop recounts an instance where a chunk of an Armenian's flesh "was cut out of his body, and jestingly offered for sale: Good fresh meat and dirt cheap!" The amused bystanders echoed, "Who'll buy fine dog's meat?" (Northrop, 1896, page 333). Harris states, "Many of the dead were left in the streets for days as food for dogs" (Harris, 1897, page 214). During the Genocide, bodies of hanged Armenians remained on public display to be "partially devoured by dogs" (Kévorkian, 2011, page 239). The letters written home from one Turkish soldier in Kharpert assures his parents and brothers he is fine, his group having "killed 1,200 Armenians, all of them as food for the dogs" (Balakian, P., 2003, page 113). Tachjian quotes the diaries of one survivor: "The poor people are all living tombs, they have no time even to protect their dead. One of the deceased died at night. During the night, a dog or cat ate his face, and they didn't even notice" (page 137, 2019; see also page 142).

Many Armenian children in orphanages succumbed to the conditions of hunger, disease, and brutality. The children desperate to stay alive made soups with the ground up bones of their friends:

> Children who were unable to withstand the blows were unceremoniously buried behind the college's former chapel. "At night," Panian went on to explain, "The jackals and wild dogs would dig them up and throw their bones here and there… at night, kids would run out to the nearby forest to get apples or any fruits they could find—and their feet would hit bones. They would take these bones back to their rooms and secretly grind them to make soup, or mix them with grain so they could eat them as there was not enough food at the orphanage. They were eating the bones of their dead friends. (Manuk-Khaloyan, n.d., page 4)

The Haroians lived in the village of Tadem, and these scenes took place in Tadem during the Massacres and the Genocide: "As for the cadavers of those hunted down in the surrounding fields, dogs, foxes, and wolves had already devoured them" (Kaloosdian, 2015, page 24). Another Tadem survivor commented on the fate of the dead: "Vultures and animals ate them …. I later saw bones. They were still there" (Kaloosdian, 2015, page 130).

Guleeg Haroian is not the only one to use the word "eat" in her oral history. She is clearly using a common metaphor. When Guleeg is hiding at a butcher's, the soldiers arrive and tell him to come with them. The butcher replies, "Your eyes should be blinded! If they opened a house in the city, how do we see it? Your tongue should be sliced. Why don't you say there is a collection? You're going to fake us out and eat us." Or, an Ottoman official to whom Guleeg Haroian goes to obtain transport to Mardin responds to her request in this manner: "He rubbed and rubbed his beard. He said, 'How can I give you protection? They ate and finished the Armenians. Now the Turks and Arabs are killing each other. I sent 30 soldiers out and two returned. They went to help someone, and they were all killed but two. They ate the rest. This is a wild place….'"

More missionaries in Turkey confirm these acts and way of thinking: "A dog will not eat a dog, one of his own kind; but the outrages, indignities, barbaric and fiendish, which these human devils heap on defenseless women and children are horrible beyond all conception" (Pierce, 1896, page 432).

The mentality persists today in Turkey. Travel writer Philip Marsden opens *The Crossing Place* with the episode that stirred his interest in the Armenians: "One summer, walking in the hills of eastern Turkey, I came across a short piece of bone. It was lodged in the rubble of a landslip and had clearly been there for many years. I rubbed its chalky surface and examined the worn bulbs of the joint; I took it to be the limb of some domestic animal and dropped it into my pocket. Beyond the rubble, the land felt away to a dusty valley which coursed down the plain of Kharput. The plain was hazy and I could just make out a truck bowling across it, kicking up a screen of pale dust in its wake. I carried on down the valley. It was a strange, still place and rounding a bluff, I stumbled on the ruins of a village. A shepherd was squatting in the shade of a tumbled-down wall, whistling. I showed him the piece of bone and gestured at the ruins around him. The shepherd nodded, wiping together his palms in an unambiguous gesture. He said simply, '*Ermeni.*' Then he took the bone and threw it to his dog." *Ermeni*: the Armenians" (page 1).

Afterword:
Genocidal Captivity and Absorption in Comparative Context —
Dr. Rebecca Jinks

Senior Lecturer in Modern History, Department of History
Royal Holloway, University of London

Guleeg and Eva's experiences, and what they further witnessed, were in many ways characteristic of the experiences of women and children during the Armenian genocide. Rape and sexual violence; forced marriage; exchanging domestic, agricultural, or industrial labor in return for protection from deportation or death; efforts to hide, or escape; the adoption of children into Turkish, Kurdish, or Arab households; and the difficulties—and certain silences—around recovery and reintegration in the aftermath. But these experiences are not unique to the Armenian genocide. Across the nineteenth and twentieth centuries indigenous children in Australia and North America were removed from their families and placed in boarding schools and mission homes, to teach them the "white man's ways" and ultimately absorb and assimilate them into the white settler population; during the "ethnic unmixing" of Partition in India in 1947, women from Muslim, Hindu and Sikh communities were abducted as their families fled for the new borders, and raped, kept behind, and forcibly married into different religious communities; and in 2014, women and children from the Yezidi religious minority in northern Iraq were kidnapped by Islamic State (IS) forces, distributed or sold to IS fighters and supporters, and kept as slaves.

We can call this phenomenon "genocidal absorption": where, rather than being killed, women and children are removed from the ethnic, religious, or national community that they are born into, as part of the process of group destruction. Unlike those cases where women are held in rape camps (Bosnia, Rwanda, Bangladesh) before being released or killed, the intent here is to physically, biologically and/or culturally absorb these women and children into the perpetrator group on a permanent basis. In the perpetrators' eyes, they thus cease to exist as Aborigines and Indians, Armenians and Yezidi, Indians (Hindu or Sikh) and Pakistani (Muslims). And as with Guleeg and Eva, in these other cases some victims also returned to their original communities—either by escaping, being located and recovered, or sometimes, many years later, seeking to rediscover their heritage and past families. Here, too, reintegration was always difficult, laden with certain silences as victims and communities navigated taboos around conversion, intermarriage, children, and the loss of cultural knowledge and language, and renegotiated identity in the aftermath of absorption.

Oral histories and written testimonies such as Guleeg and Eva's are key to accessing and understanding the experience of genocidal absorption, as scholars working on the above cases have also observed (Menon and Bhasin, 1998; Butalia, 2000; Attwood, 2001; Woolford, 2015, pages 50-56; see also Saikia, 2011). The official record—state archives, diplomatic sources, political observers—is useful because it allows us to understand the ideologies, the fears, and the genocidal fantasies of political elites, the decisions of leaders, and the development and implementation of genocidal policies. But only rarely does it record the impact of such events on its victims, and even more rarely still are women's voices included. Written and oral testimonies are essential in filling in this missing part of history. In the process of telling us their stories, the victims allow us to understand the group and individual repercussions of genocidal absorption, and to understand that the process was much more varied than we might otherwise expect. They show us that the victims were not just passive but, like Guleeg, exercised extraordinary agency in the face of a crushing, all-encompassing campaign of genocide.

They can also give us a rare glimpse into the behavior and motivations of "ordinary" perpetrators (who likewise appear only infrequently in official archives). Oral histories of genocidal absorption are, of course, not without their difficulties. Much depends on the relationship between the interviewer and interviewee, including when the listener is a family member. Regardless of this relationship, because of taboos over rape, intermarriage, and purity, survivors often choose to "pass over" difficult and taboo experiences (like Guleeg did), or, as Nighat Said Khan found in speaking with Indian women abductees, women might describe such violence fully but in the third person—instances which they said they had seen or heard about, not things which had happened to them (Khan, 2011, page 134). For survivors who later re-joined their original communities, certain silences or presentation of their experiences may be necessary to avoid suspicions about their loyalties or purity in the present. And, of course, oral histories of genocidal absorption have to contend with the fact that survivors are remembering for us extreme and bewildering experiences which frequently lasted for years but were punctuated with clearly remembered moments of loss, violence, abduction, or realization: their recall can be fragmentary, dis-ordered, and blurry. But all of these silences, clearly remembered moments, inclusions, and fragments can themselves tell us a lot about the experience of genocidal absorption.

These other cases—Australia, North America, India, and Iraq—can help us better understand the Armenian experience. There are, of course, clear differences among them: for example, some perpetrators envisaged full-scale biological absorption, others prioritized cultural assimilation, others sought permanent servitude for the victim group. In some cases, the fault-line was religion, in others race or ethnicity. But comparing them demonstrates to us that the intention in each case was *the demographic disappearance of the group* – and that absorption was a means of disappearance alongside killing which also, frequently, had economic and other benefits for the perpetrator group. Comparison also shows us that there was no universal experience of absorption (or recovery), and that many of the victims' strategies of resistance (or submission)—and difficulties of reintegration—recur across the centuries. The rest of this afterword will discuss the cases in turn, beginning with the Armenian genocide, to draw out these parallels and differences.

Guleeg and Eva's experiences were multifaceted and give us a real insight into different experiences of genocidal absorption during the Armenian genocide. In the villages and towns of Ottoman Turkey, they were far from the ruling Committee of Union and Progress' (CUP) deliberations and decision-making. But over the spring and early summer of 1915, CUP decisions altered their lives radically. In the context of heavy defeats on the Russian front, and anticipated Allied attacks on the coast, CUP fears of Armenian nationalist ambitions and their potential to become a fifth column escalated into a series of orders to empty the Armenian heartlands of Armenians: to make them demographically disappear, in the service of making a new Ottoman Turkish nation. The murder of Armenian men (either outside villages and towns, or through forced labor in the Ottoman military) was one way of neutralizing this threat, and also had the effect of leaving Armenian women to cope alone—if, like Guleeg, they were not already doing so. The majority of Armenian women and children were murdered during the deportations, through brutal violence, exhaustion, starvation, and disease—but at least 100,000 (Sarafian, 2010) were absorbed into Turkish, Kurdish, or Arab households. The CUP elites tolerated a certain measure of this in part because women and children were thought to have more malleable identities and be easier to convert to Islam; demographically insignificant, they would be fully integrated within a generation. Some women and children were absorbed in their own villages, like Guleeg and some of her neighbors. Others were snatched en route, given up by their families, or picked up as they lay exhausted or dying by the side of the deportation route (Sarafian 2010). Some children ended up in orphanages (such as the Red Cross facilities that Guleeg brought children to when she found them begging in the streets after the war) (see e.g., Panian, 2015).

From testimonies like Guleeg and Eva's, we get a sense of how some Armenians were able to evade capture and/or deportation, and to resist and accommodate certain aspects of absorption. While it was standard to change Armenians' names (as Eva's was changed to Shofkeeah), convert them to Islam, and change their clothing, many survivors over a certain age remembered their names, and tried to quietly hold on to their language and religious identity. From their testimonies we also get a sense of the diverse motives of the Turks, Kurds, and Arabs who took them in. People from all walks of life absorbed Armenians, from the local police chief down to ordinary villagers. There are many stories of Turkish neighbors, acquaintances, or housekeepers saving individual Armenian children or sometimes larger families from deportation; further down the deportation routes, complete strangers would sometimes take in Armenians who were ill, or because their families begged them to save their children. Others had far less altruistic motives. But all ultimately benefitted economically: Armenians performed domestic and/or sexual labor for all of these households; for poorer families, marrying a son to an Armenian girl saved on the price of a dowry, a major expense for an Ottoman family; if an Armenian boy was the sole survivor of his family, what remained of the family property often passed to him and thence to his new head of household. Guleeg's testimony recounts various episodes of working for Turks, or paying for protection as she says, "I went to that same *khanum*. She would keep a few different Armenians at a time. She took the gold and said, 'I will save you.' They sent me working in the fields" (page 45). Some Armenians were treated well, some horribly abused; some were given daily reminders of their difference, and some more or less fully absorbed, such that they became part of the family. These differences affected the question of escape, rescue, and recovery after the war. Some Armenians, feeling happy in their new families – and safe from the dangers that being Armenian had brought them – did not want to leave or, slightly differently, were nervous about rejoining the Armenian community because they anticipated being shamed. Others escaped as soon as they could. Some were willingly or forcibly recovered, by one of the various international and Armenian humanitarian organizations working to rebuild the Armenian community after the war (one of which Guleeg worked for). Those with children born of their time in a Muslim household had an especially difficult choice: children were supposed to remain with the father, and the Armenian community could be especially hesitant about these children. Reintegration, then, could sometimes be a smooth process – but as we see with Guleeg's decision not to tell her husband about her two forced marriages, that smoothness was sometimes dependent on and sustained by silences, both within families and also the wider community as it sought to rebuild itself.

Genocide and genocidal absorption in Australia and North America took a rather different form, largely because of their settler colonial nature: here genocide took place over centuries, and entire continents. While there has been strong political resistance from the white settler populations of Australia and North America to considering the process of settler-colonization *as* genocide, there is now a considerable body of academic scholarship exploring the colonizers' genocidal fantasies and actions across time and space (e.g. Madley, 2015; Moses, 2004). In their early stages, both were characterized by frontier violence, the dispossession and removal of indigenous peoples, and the establishment of reservations. But in the late nineteenth and early twentieth centuries, these practices of physical extermination and segregation gradually gave way to policies of assimilation and absorption.

In Australia around 1900, roughly 60,000 of the original c.300,000 indigenous peoples had survived the nineteenth-century dispossession and frontier violence, as white colonists spread across the continent (Manne, 2004, page 226). Thanks to the Darwinian notion of "survival of the fittest," white Australians believed that Aboriginal populations were destined slowly to die out. But the spread of settlers had produced a new "problem": the rape of Aboriginal women by white settlers had produced thousands of "half-caste" children. And these children were not dying out – in fact their numbers were increasing. Their half-European blood meant that many settlers felt it unconscionable to leave them in what they considered the "filthy, immoral, superstitious, degraded Aboriginal world" (Manne, 2004, page 225), and considered them salvageable for inclusion in white society.

Thus, while child removal (largely for the purposes of labor) had happened since the early days of white settlement (Haebich, 2000, pages 65-130), over the early decades of the twentieth century a system of half-caste child removal developed in Australia (with Western Australia and the Northern Territories at the epicenter). Half-Aboriginal children were taken to state-run or mission institutions, the purpose of which was to isolate them completely from their original communities, give them rudimentary education and training, and prepare them for life among the European population, "as manual laborers or station hands if they were boys, and as cheap domestic servants, for which there was an insatiable demand, if they were girls" (Manne, 2004, page 224). They were banned from speaking their own language and Christianized. They were taken without warning in an often hugely traumatic process, and without the parents being told where they were going; their names were often changed, and bureaucratic barriers put in the way of either children or parents ever locating each other again. Over the 1920s and 1930s, policymakers and bureaucrats articulated a theory of "breeding out the black": by intermarrying these "lighter-skinned" children only with whites or other half-Aboriginals, the half-caste children would eventually become absorbed into the white population. In the words of A.O. Neville, Chief Protector of Aborigines in Western Australia: after fifty years, everyone would "be able to forget that there ever were any Aborigines in Australia" (Manne, 2004, page 237). After the Holocaust, different sensitivities about the potential of eugenicist policies prompted a shift in Australian policy, where all Aboriginals were now to be absorbed into white Australian society (a more expansive "solution" to a more expansive version of the same "problem"). Children were still removed and placed in institutions well into the 1970s—in fact in larger numbers than before (Manne, 2004, page 239)—but with the goal of economic and cultural assimilation, rather than biological absorption. While the pre- and post-World War Two policies were conceptually distinct, as Anna Haebich comments, "assimilation determines conformity to the dominant culture while it erases others. Removing children from their families to institutions to be assimilated drove ongoing dispossession, cut transmission of knowledge and culture down the generations, and contributed to elimination of local populations by preventing their reproduction" (Haebich, 2015/16, page 21).

The 1997 *Bringing Them Home* report, the outcome of a National Inquiry into Aboriginal child removal, demonstrated well the heart-rending impact of the removal system on the children. The report argued that genocide had taken place, referring to clause 2(e) of the United Nations Genocide Convention, which defines the transfer of children from one group to another as an act of genocide. It was the extracts of oral testimonies with children who had been taken and absorbed—the so-called Stolen Generations—which had the most public impact (Attwood, 2001). Collectively, these testimonies detail the variety of experiences the Stolen Generations had across multiple institutions and decades, where they endured the bewildering experience of acculturation into white life patterns and the suppression of Aboriginal ones, and different forms of physical, mental, and bureaucratic abuse. They were particularly vulnerable to exploitation and violence when sent out into the labor market, and those adopted out into white families (which became more common after 1945) sometimes landed in living and supportive homes, and others abusive environments. Many describe the ways in which, while outwardly appearing to represent "successful" integration into white society, they never really "fitted" – either because of daily encounters with racism or because of an unsettling feeling of dislocation and disconnection with their original identity. One stolen child, Julie Lavelle, observed that (white people) would often draw a contrast between the Aboriginal community she was taken from, "with all that despair and hopelessness", and the advantages her wealthy white parents gave her: "Yes, I do have all those things, and that is OK, but there's no way that that was ever a trade-off for not having known my mother—I have no memory of her—of not having my own identity, of not knowing for thirty-two years of my life that I had biological brothers and sisters" (*Australian Human Rights Commission*, 1997). For those who managed to locate their original families – often only after protracted battle with bureaucratic systems designed to prevent reunions – the yawning gap in cultural knowledge and experience of their Aboriginal heritage, and their feeling of being neither white nor Aboriginal, made reconnecting extremely difficult, and acceptance sometimes difficult for their original community.

Similar ideas of biological and cultural assimilation began to circulate in North America towards the end of the nineteenth century. By the time white settlers reached the west coast of what became the United States of America and Canada, the wars and forced removal of Indian tribes to reservations, which had characterized the previous centuries of "engagement" with "the Indian problem," had become extremely expensive. Although disease, massacres, and genocides of at least some Native American groups had decimated their populations – in the United States, from approximately 5,000,000 to roughly 240,000 by the last decades of the nineteenth century – and some white settlers still believed that Native Americans were destined to die out, "the Indian problem" remained (Madley, 2015). Towards the end of the nineteenth century, both states gradually shifted the "strategy of elimination" from physical mechanisms (killing or confinement to reservations) to legal mechanisms, and cultural and biological assimilation into settler society. In the US, new legal definitions of Indianness acted to limit their number (and thus the financial and legal obligations of the state towards them, as agreed in previous treaties): by defining an Indian as a person with at least one quarter Indian blood, and allowing intermarriage to proceed as it had for centuries, eventually Indians would be "defined out of existence" (Limerick in Ellinghaus, 2009, page 62). The 1887 Dawes Act struck at the few remaining foundations of Native American social and cultural life: Indian Reservations, which until then had been held as common land and as such allowed a semblance of traditional communal life, were henceforth to be divided into individual allotments, on which nuclear Indian families were expected to become self-supporting farmers—thus, forcibly integrated into the American dream. Similar ideas were circulating in Canada, where one official, Duncan Campbell Scott, felt that "[t]he happiest future for the Indian race is absorption into the general population, and this is the object of the policy of our government." Scott, who later played a significant role in the design of Indian policy and residential schools in Canada, hoped that "[t]he great forces of intermarriage and education will finally overcome the lingering traces of native custom and tradition" (Palmater, 2014, page 31).

This faith in education as a solution set the stage for child removal on a large scale on both sides of the border. While there had been sporadic and disorganized efforts to establish schools for indigenous children beforehand (Woolford, 2015, pages 50-56), by 1879 boarding schools began to be seen as the most effective model for "civilizing"—assimilating—Indians. Adults were thought to be too stubborn in their traditions for effective assimilation, but children were thought to be more impressionable and assimilable. The ambition of officials on both sides of the border was to remove as many children as possible to boarding schools, ideally at some distance from the reservation. Parental consent was desirable, but in the United States, for example, agents of the Bureau of Indian Affairs were permitted to "withhold rations, clothing and other annuities from Indian parents or guardians who refuse or neglect to send and keep their children of proper school age in school" (Churchill, 2004b, page 88). Many children were kept at school for ten years or more, and not permitted to return home at weekends or during the short summer break. 'Europeanization" was rapid, and brutal. They were prohibited from speaking their own languages or practicing Indigenous spirituality—a ban which necessitated constant surveillance on the part of the school officials, and punishment for infractions; their hair was cut, in violation of indigenous cultural practices, and their clothing changed to European styles. Dormitories were laid out barracks-style, and their daily schedules were rigidly organized, punctuated by the ringing of a school bell to signal time for waking, praying, eating, learning, and sleeping—a rigidity in sharp contrast to indigenous patterns of life. Students were taught patriotism, obedience, and Christianity. In the words of one First Nations student in Canada who gave an oral deposition to the Truth and Reconciliation Commission, "As soon as we got in there, the beatings started right away. You know when, like, well first it was humiliating, they'd cut your hair off, and put a bowl on your head, and told you to take your clothes off, and they threw flea powder all over you, and then they'd tell you to go up to have a shower right after that, and that was pretty humiliating. But right away, man, the beatings started 'cause most kids didn't know what the rules were or anything like that, eh. And if you didn't follow the rules, that was it, you'd get strapped with the strap" (quoted in Woolford, 2015, page 189). Punishment and violence were commonplace, and the low state funding ensured that students often went hungry and were obliged to do a lot of the manual labor needed around the schools to save on costs (Churchill, 2004b, pages 90-100). All of this was designed, in the words of one prominent school leader, to "kill the Indian, save the man" (Churchill, 2004a). The experiences of the children varied, of course, depending upon the time period, the individual school and its staff, the distance from home (which sometimes meant that running away or parental intervention was possible), and how strongly a child resisted or tried to subvert assimilation (Woolford, 2015). In Canada, the state mostly subcontracted its residential school system to missionary organizations, and the system itself was generally more effective at keeping more children away from home, for longer. In the United States, boarding schools were mostly federally-run, and reforms in the 1930s changed the experience somewhat. But the outcome was similar for many children: taught to hate their Indian identity and culture, estrangement from their original communities followed. They were often regarded with some suspicion by their original communities, and their loss of indigenous knowledge, learning, and culture inhibited a full return to indigenous life. Tellingly, alumni of the boarding schools often ended up marrying each other, completing the absorptionist and assimilationist goals of the schooling system (Ellinghaus, 2009, page 69).

The violence which accompanied the Partition of India in 1947 brought absorption and assimilation of a different sort. During the complex process of India's transition to independence from British rule, the main political players' inability to resolve the question of India's future political organization allowed the demands that had been emanating from more militant quarters for a separate homeland for India's Muslim population to gradually take hold, and Partition to become inevitable. India was split into Muslim-majority areas (which became East and West Pakistan) and Hindu and Sikh-majority areas (which became India): this necessitated drawing a line through the particularly-mixed provinces of Punjab and Bengal. Intercommunal violence began around the country even before the official boundaries were drawn, carefully fostered by local state and non-state actors and groups, in an escalating process whereby violence against one community spurred anticipatory and retributive violence from others (Jana, 2022; Khan, 2017). Fearing this violence, and what it might mean to end up in a new nation into which they did not "fit," roughly eight million people (largely in Punjab and Bengal) packed up their families, left behind their homes, and fled across the new borders. The refugees were accompanied by military escorts as far as possible, but the journeys were still hazardous, traumatic, and beset by lethal violence. Roughly half a million people were killed: convoys were ambushed, families separated, children orphaned, and about 75,000 women were abducted (Menon and Bhasin, 1993, page WS3).

The abductions were part of this "brutal logic of reprisal," and also served to hasten the departure of families who had not yet left. They were accompanied by a kind of exultation and excess (familiar in some descriptions of Armenian women's experiences): not just rape, but extremely public rape, and bodily mutilation (Menon and Bhasin, 1998, pages 38, 41-43). They were "simultaneously an assertion of identity and a humiliation of the rival community…. When accompanied by the forcible conversion and marriage, it could be counted upon to outrage both family and community honor and religious sentiments" (Menon and Bhasin, 1993, page WS3). The demographic profile, and experiences, of these women varied widely. Most were below 35, and primarily from rural backgrounds. Some were separated from their family or village group, and taken; sometimes the men of the village were massacred, and the women taken; some were left behind by their families as hostages; some were sold and changed hands several times; others were protected from that, and incorporated into their new families; very many were converted and lived with considerable dignity and respect. As Ritu Menon and Kamla Bhasin argue, "it would be false to presume that their lot was uniformly grim, their 'abductors' without exception 'bestial' or unreliable and craven…" (Menon and Bhasin, 1993, page WS5). At the same time, the economic value that the women provided—primarily as domestic labor—was also evident, and particularly important to refugee families. As with the Armenian genocide, then, absorption happened for a mix of motives.

Oral histories of abduction and the post-Partition recovery effort confirm that not all of the abducted women led "grim" lives. After Partition, the new states of India and Pakistan agreed to mount a "recovery operation," eventually in force between 1948 and 1956, which envisaged local police and social workers locating and returning abducted women to their families. But this process of "return" and "reintegration" was fraught and in many ways remained incomplete. Not all women wanted to return: one social worker accompanying 21 women who had been located and were being returned to India, reported that the women pleaded with her to leave them behind, asking: "Why are you destroying our lives?" (Menon and Bhasin, 1993, page WS6). Their reluctance to return was in some cases because they antici-pated that their families would not want them back, "dishonored"—often a correct assumption, as it turned out. Sometimes they were happy where they were: some had taken advantage of the turmoil to marry outside their religious group, which would not have been ordinarily permitted, and others had become happy with their lives. Indeed, one woman refused to return because she was pregnant; she commanded a lot of local respect and was not forced to participate in Islam. But despite the women's reluctance or fears of rejection, they were recovered and returned anyway: as Menon and Bhasin write, for the Indian state particularly, "it seemed that the only answer to forcible conversion was forcible recovery" (Menon and Bhasin, 1993, page WS11). Neither was the reintegration of abducted women a smooth process: some families rejected them (and some rejected their families), the issue of children proved particularly difficult (many were compelled to leave their children behind, and the state performed abortions on others), and while some were able to marry and reintegrate into their communities, large numbers of abducted women lived in state-supported camps and group accommodation for the rest of their lives.

The fall of the Saddam regime in 2003 made the position of the Yezidi in Iraq more precarious, as for all minorities (Schmidinger, 2022, pages 52-63). As society broke down, the Yezidi were increasingly attacked by extremist groups, including the group which would later become Islamic State (IS). In part these attacks were ideologically-derived: IS did not consider Yezidi "people of the book," viewing them as "infidels" not worthy of the relative protection that Christians and Jews deserved. After IS gained control first of Raqqa in Syria in January 2014, then Mosul in Iraq later that June, their next step was to consolidate the territory in between, the Nineveh plain. A high concentration of Yezidi lives on the Nineveh plain, around the town of Sinjar. In the early hours of August 3rd 2014, IS launched a coordinated attack against the Sinjar region, which lasted four or five weeks. Roughly 250,000 Yezidi fled to the relative safety of Sinjar mountain, but not all left quickly enough. For the 10,000 who did not escape, in some villages they were offered the option to convert to Islam; in other villages they were not. Where religious conversion was refused, or not offered, IS followed a pattern of attack highly reminiscent of the Armenian genocide. The men were separated and killed. The women and children were loaded onto buses and taken to the cities of Mosul or Tel Afar. The young boys were usually absorbed into IS fighting units as child soldiers. About a fifth of the women were given to IS fighters as a reward, and the rest sold or forcibly married to IS fighters. There they were designated "sabaya," slaves, and IS ideologues issued explicit religious justification for their rape, enslavement, and status as property. They were forced to convert to Islam, were often sold and resold, and suffered extremely brutal treatment. In this case, then, the women were absorbed into IS but only to occupy the lowest strata of the IS hierarchy; they were valuable for their forced sexual and domestic labor, and as an incentive for IS fighters to join or to outdo themselves on the battlefield, but never intended for assimilation (Schmidinger, 2022, page 78, 86).

Slowly, Yezidi women began to manage to escape, often by taking advantage of a lax moment in their captors' attention. They were aided by smuggling networks; typically, a woman would manage to call a relative or friend, who would then organize rescue by one of a number of subterranean networks. Sometimes they were aided by local non-IS Iraqis. Sometimes they were literally bought back by their families or community (see e.g. Mikhail, 2018). But the fear of rejection was strong: even more strongly than in the Armenian community in 1915, intermarriage, rape, and religious conversion were completely taboo in Iraqi Yezidi society. The abducted women were all too aware of this, as were IS fighters, who would frequently taunt the women that they would never be re-accepted into the refugee Yezidi community (Fischer and Zagros, 2019, page 209). However, in the wake of the genocide, the Yezidi community performed a remarkable about-turn from its previous practices. In February 2015, the religious leader of the Yezidi, the Baba Sheikh, issued a decree which affirmed that the survivors would be re-accepted into the Yezidi community (Fischer and Zagros, 2019, page 210). The Baba Sheikh was responding to various pressures—various other community leaders have claimed that it was their idea, which they encouraged him to pursue, but it is also clear that families were working to rescue, and re-accepting, their daughters before the decree appeared (McGee, 2018, page 91). And while the process of re-acceptance appears reasonably smooth, some survivors report that "they accept us, but they don't respect us" (Bor, 2019). And for many, here, too, the issue of children conceived while in captivity still sharply divides the community—producing very difficult choices and much anguish for the Yezidi mothers.

Thinking about different case studies together, as above, allows us to highlight emerging patterns—and shows very clearly that experiences of the same phenomenon can differ wildly. Likewise, one of the really precious things about oral histories (and written testimonies) is that they give us an on-the-ground perspective of what happened to one individual, who also observes what happened to others. Oral history guards against making generalizations: every experience is different. Thus, the stereotyped images that we have of women being "carried off" or snatched, screaming, are true of some victims – but not all. Stereotypes of cruel, vicious perpetrators are true of some—but not all. Stereotypes of victims as completely helpless and passive are almost never true. Stereotypes prevent us from seeing the very human experience that is genocide: oral histories confront us with it.

At the same time, the case studies above demonstrate certain common-alities to the phenomenon of genocidal absorption. The first is to note that in each case, the overriding goal of the genocidal elites is the destruction of the victim group—its removal from their territory. Alongside other methods like killing, absorption is one method to achieve the disappearance of the victim group—whether biologically, culturally, or by turning women into slaves. And those genocidal elites are no doubt aware of the value (financial or sexual) of these women and children to some ordinary people, and that this can encourage them to join in with the genocidal campaign. But oral histories—like Guleeg and Eva's—show us that not all those who absorbed victims made such calculations. Instead, a complex mix of reasons lay behind each absorption: economic or sexual value; a kind of glee or exultation as the normal rules of life were suspended; retribution; altruism; affection for neighbors or acquaintances. And even if economic reasons were not a primary motivator, households almost always benefitted from the labor or economic value of those they absorbed.

Second is to note the victims' agency and resistance efforts. A very striking tactic which recurs across the Armenian, Indian, and Yezidi cases is that women covered their faces with mud or dirt to appear unattractive (see Menon and Bhasin, 1998, page 58; Otten, 2017). In each case, victims tried to escape—like Guleeg, or indigenous children who ran away from residential schools (Woolford, 2015, pages 132-137), or Yezidi women who managed to get hold of a cell phone. Others kept their original identities alive in some way or another (speaking their own language quietly, maintaining a network with other absorbed victims nearby, or resisting or subverting efforts to change their religion). Indeed, despite wholesale efforts to change (variously) the victims' names, clothing, language, religion, and life patterns, what is striking is how *ineffective* absorption was in changing the victims' identities and culture—especially when so many faced daily reminders of their original identity.

Finally—mirroring the previous point—the case studies above remind us that "return" and "reintegration" were also often "incomplete." Given their experiences, it would be impossible for absorbed women and children to simply return to their original communities, as if nothing had happened. For those who did not have wholly horrendous experiences, who retained a fondness for some of the family who absorbed them or parts of their culture, a wholesale rejection of that identity and experience would have been difficult. And some, of course, did not want to return, even if forced to. Attitudes varied in Armenian, indigenous, Indian and Pakistani, and Yezidi communities, and perfectly understandable, but difficult, questions of purity and identity were opened up by reintegration, especially around children. On these issues, oral testimonies tend to be most silent: assumptions, norms, and taboos within a community about gender and belonging deeply affect how stories of genocidal absorption are told, many years later, once the survivors have returned "home."

REFERENCES

Australian Human Rights Commission. *Bringing Them Home: Separation of Aboriginal and Torres Strait Islander Children from their Families.* DVD, 1997. Available on Youtube: https://www.youtube.com/watch?v=Sl82VMuuKI0

Attwood, Bain. "Learning about the Truth: The Stolen Generations Narrative." In *Telling Stories: Indigenous History and Memory in Australia and New Zealand.* Eds. Bain Attwood and Fiona Magowan. Allen and Unwin. Crows Nest: 2001. Pages 183-212.

Bor, Güley. "Community-Level Stigma Faced by Female Yezidi and Shi'a Turkmen Survivors of CRSV in Iraq." LSE Middle East Centre blog, June 19th, 2019. Available at: https://blogs.lse.ac.uk/mec/2019/06/19/

stigma-faced-by-female-yazidi-and-shia-turkmen-survivors-of-crsv-in-iraq/

Butalia, Urvashi. *The Other Side of Silence: Voices from the Partition of India*. Duke University Press. Durham, NC: 2000.

Churchill, Ward. *Kill the Indian, Save the Man: The Genocidal Impact of Indian Reservation Schools*. City Lights Publishers. San Francisco, CA: 2004a.

Churchill, Ward. "Genocide By Any Other Name: North American Residential Schools in Context." In *Genocide, War Crimes and the West: History and Complicity*. Ed. Adam Jones. Zed books. London: 2004b. Pages 78-115.

Ellinghaus, Katherine. "Biological Absorption and Genocide: A Comparison of Indigenous Assimilation Policies in the United States and Australia." *Genocide Studies and Prevention*. 4:1. 2009. Pages 59-79.

Fischer, Tyler, and Zagros, Nahro. "Yezidi Baptism and Rebaptism: Resilience, Reintegration, and Religious Adaptation." In *Routledge Handbook on the Kurds*. Ed. Michael M. Gunter. Routledge. Abingdon, UK: 2019. Pages 202-214.

Haebich, Anna. *Broken Circles: Fragmenting Indigenous Families, 1800-2000*. Fremantle Arts Center Press. Fremantle: 2000.

Haebich, Anna. "Neoliberalism, Settler Colonialism and the History of Indigenous Child Removal in Australia." *Australian Indigenous Law Review*. 19:1. 2015/2016. Pages 20-31.

Jana, Sayantani. "Decolonization and Genocide: Re-Examining Indian Partition, 1946-1947." *Holocaust and Genocide Studies*. 36:3. 2022. Pages 334-352.

Khan, Nighat Said. "Identity, Violence and Women: A Reflection on the Partition of India 1947." In *Perspectives on Modern South Asia: A Reader in Culture, History and Representation*. Ed. Kamala Visweswaran. Blackwell Publishing. Oxford: 2011. Pages 134-8.

Khan, Yasmin. *The Great Partition: The Making of India and Pakistan.* 2nd edition. Yale University Press. New Haven, CT: 2017.

Madley, Benjamin. "Reexamining the American Genocide Debate: Meaning, Historiography, and New Methods." *American Historical Review.* 120:1. 2015. Pages 98-139.

Manne, Robert. "Aboriginal Child Removal and the Question of Genocide, 1900-1940." In *Genocide and Settler Society: Frontier Violence and Stolen Indigenous Children in Australian History.* Ed. A. Dirk Moses. Berghahn Books. New York: 2004.

McGee, Thomas. "Saving the survivors: Yezidi women, Islamic State and the German Admissions Programme." *Kurdish Studies.* 6:1. 2018. Pages 85-109.

Menon, Ritu, and Bhasin, Kamla. *Borders and Boundaries: Women in India's Partition.* Rutgers University Press. New Brunswick, NJ: 1998.

Menon, Ritu, and Bhasin, Kamla. "Recovery, Rupture, Resistance: Indian State and Abduction of Women during Partition." *Economic and Political Weekly.* 28:17. 1993. Pages WS2-WS11.

Mikhail, Dunya. *The Beekeper of Sinjar.* Serpent's Tail. London: 2018.

Moses, Dirk A., ed. *Genocide and Settler Society: Frontier Violence and Stolen Indigenous Children in Australian History.* Berghahn Books. New York: 2004.

Otten, Cathy. *With Ash on their Faces: Yezidi Women and the Islamic State.* OR Books. New York: 2017.

Palmater, Pamela. "Genocide, Indian Policy, and Legislated Elimination of Indians in Canada." *Aboriginal Policy Studies.* 3:3. 2014. Pages 27-54.

Panian, Karnig. *Goodbye, Antoura: A Memoir of the Armenian Genocide.* Stanford University Press. Stanford, CA: 2015.

Saikia, Yasmin, *Women, War and the Making of Bangladesh: Remembering 1971.* Duke University Press. Durham, NC: 2011.

Sarafian, Ara. "The Absorption of Armenian Women and Children Into Muslim Households as a Structural Component of the Armenian Genocide." In *In God's Name: Genocide and Religion in the Twentieth Century*. Eds. Omer Bartov and Phyllis Mack. Berghahn Books. New York: 2010. Pages 209-21.

Schmidinger, Thomas. *The World Has Forgotten Us: Sinjar and the Islamic State's Genocide of the Yezidis*. Pluto. London: 2022.

Woolford, Andrew. *This Benevolent Experiment: Indigenous Boarding Schools, Genocide, and Redress in Canada and the United States*. University of Nebraska Press. Lincoln, NE: 2015.

Photographs

Guleeg Haroian with her husband Hagop (seated) and her daughters Eva and Mary (infant, born in America)

Քէռիս, Եղբայրս խաչատուր եւ Ես. Քոյս՝ Ասատուրը, Կուլիկը,
բրորդիս Եղսան

THE FAMILY BEFORE THE 1915 ARMENIAN GENOCIDE. GULEEG HAROIAN STANDS IN
THE MIDDLE OF THE BACK ROW. THE BOY WEARING A FEZ (LEFT) IS BEDROS HAROIAN,
WHO WOULD SURVIVE TO WRITE MEMOIRS OF A SOLDIER ABOUT THE DAYS OF TRAGEDY
(TADEM PRESS, 2021). THE INFANT ON THE KNEES OF THE MAN (LEFT) IS EVA. THE SMALL
GIRL STANDING BETWEEN THE LEGS OF THE MAN (RIGHT) IS MARY HAROIAN, WHO
WOULD DIE DURING THE GENOCIDE.

Editor's Note:
A Legacy of Good

Guleeg Haroian's life in America spanned close to six decades. Reunited with her husband, Guleeg had two new children: Mary Tashjian (née Haroian) and Rose Guerin (née Haroian).

GULEEG HAROIAN WITH HER TWO TEENAGE DAUGHTERS, ROSE (LEFT) AND MARY (RIGHT), IN AMERICA.

Guleeg Haroian's family of three children—Eva, Mary, and Rose—grew into six grandchildren, fourteen great-grandchildren, fifteen great-great grandchildren, and now a growing number of great-great-great grandchildren.

Her life was ever active.

In June 1953, a powerful and destructive tornado struck her new home: Worcester, Massachusetts. The supercell levelled neighborhoods. The path of the Worcester Tornado sped directly toward my grandmother's home. She lived across the street from Assumption Preparatory School. The Worcester Tornado wrecked three floors of the building's three-foot thick brick walls, killed one priest and two nuns, and wounded many more.

That afternoon, my sixty-eight-year-old grandmother was babysitting a grandchild: Thomas Tashjian, born to Mary Tashjian (née Haroian). Guleeg was in the back yard hanging clothes as Thomas took a nap in his crib. She saw the massive tornado over the top of Assumption Preparatory School. Guleeg ran inside and up the back stairs of their three-decker home. She was between the 2nd and 3rd floor when the tornado hit. Guleeg could hear her grandchild crying in the rubble, but she could not get to him, and she began crying out in Armenian for her baby. The neighbors heard, and the man next door was ready to come over, but his wife held him back. Brother Richard Richards was walking down the street from the Assumption Brother's house, on his way down to the monastery to see if anyone needed help. Brother Richards heard Guleeg Haroian's cries and went into the basement of the house. He found Thomas pinned between two beams with his crib mattress folded over him like a peanut butter sandwich. Brother Richards pulled Thomas out, saving his life.

Thomas, Guleeg Haroian's oldest living grandchild, thrived, and he offered many recollections of his grandmother. "Gramma would come over our house, walking over from her house sucking on a raw egg, and once in our house make coffee by putting the grinds in a pan and boiling it while she found and smoked one of Dad's Pall-malls over the sink before waking Tim and I up for school. Gramma was older and for some reason had gone to the doctor, who told her she needed to get some exercise at her age. The next blizzardy morning the routine was different. I looked out through the blowing snow and could see snow flying as Gramma shoveled a path to our house. Then instead of coming in right away, she shoveled a space in front of the basketball hoop in the driveway and began throwing Tim's basketball. …she was going to make sure she kept herself strong."

Thomas' memories focus on her strength amid storms: "One day in the winter, we were sent home in the middle of a blizzard. All the Catholic kids stopped off at the Holy Rosary Church to wait for their big brothers and sisters to bring them home in the white out. I had to struggle home against the wind. I was frozen and couldn't see. Then, out of the white, I saw a dark figure… It was my Grammy walking down the street in her black dress and shawl to rescue me and bring me home. (Tashjian, 17 – 19 December 2022)

Was Guleeg Haroian ever still?

The first idea of beauty came to me through my grandmother. In the mornings, she would braid her snow-white hair and wrap the soft braids around her head. Then she would go outside to tend a garden with the flowers of New England: surges of purple iris and starbursts of day lilies the color of pumpkin infused with gold. Abundant were self-seeded wildflowers: bunches of buttercups, sprays of violets, and sometimes a lily of the valley with its tiny white bells. The blanket of petals perfumed the air. Center front was a cluster of the one flower not native to New England: big orange poppies of the Ottoman Empire floating against the summer blue day.

My grandmother would gaze at the poppies, and, following her gaze, that rush of orange entranced me. She protected those poppies in a singular way, so only when she was not looking, could I touch the silky petals and wonder at the shiny black circle inside. It was rare I could get that close to her poppies, for my grandmother had a sharp eye, I was an unruly child, and she knew it. Yet I wanted to see inside her silent gaze by peering in the big taffeta cup of orange petals.

What was she thinking during those gazes at her poppies? Those still moments in the summer blue of New England? Were these living flowers her sole connection to a distant world she had loved before it was crushed? Everything had been taken from her. She arrived in America with new clothes and a fancy new hat. Yet somehow, she had found the seeds for these orange pompoms of her native land. In the grace of that orange silk, did she recall the soft laughter of her little girls Elizabeth and Mary? In the gush of orange, did she see the poppies before the door that Hagop opened for her as a new bride? In the cloud of orange poppies dancing in the wind, did her heart pound as she almost felt the brush of her father's stubble against her young cheek?

Mary Haroian

MARY HAROIAN IN UNIFORM, W.W. II

After Mary served the United States in the Navy during WW II, she enrolled in and graduated from Clark University with a BA and MA in Psychology. She obtained her psychologist license and worked as one of the first psychologists in the State Service with the Travelling School Clinic of Grafton State Hospital, travelling to different schools and evaluating children and their problems. She left that career after marrying to start a family and work alongside her husband, Aram, a pharmacist who had launched his own business: Brittan Pharmacy. Mary Haroian retired from Brittan Pharmacy with her husband in 1988. She said to me: "I am going to walk over to Quinsigamond Community College to see if I can teach psychology or enroll in computer science courses. I am only seventy. I need to find a new career for the next twenty years." Mary began teaching psychology at Quinsigamond Community College until she retired at the age of 90 in December 2010. After retiring from the professional work at 90, Mary cooked a monthly Thursday luncheon for the Armenian Church of the Martyrs.

Rose Haroian in uniform

ROSE HAROIAN IN UNIFORM, W.W. II

After Rose Haroian served in the Navy during World War II, she earned her undergraduate degree from Marietta College and a master's degree from Boston University, where she validated the Mansur Speech Sound Discrimination Test (which became the Boston University Speech Sound Discrimination Test), and which has been used throughout the nation in early childhood education. She went on to earn a Ph.D. in Education Administration from Boston College, where she created the Haroian Early Language Picture Test for deaf children.

Rose raised her own family while successfully becoming a professor at Worcester State College, where she founded the College's highly successful Communication Disorders Clinic, now the Speech, Language, and Hearing Clinic that serves the entire central Massachusetts area. Upon retirement, Rose received the College's Professor Emeritus Award and a memorial plaque in her honor was installed in the clinic. The College created The Dr. Rose D. Haroian Endowed Scholarship to continue her legacy of excellence and of service to others.

Post-retirement, she embarked on a second career as a writer for Digital Equipment Corporation, where she was on the team that wrote the original drafts of the "All-In-One" Computer Office Automation Software Program that was used in major government and business institutions throughout the U.S. She also taught at Quinsigamond Community College, where she developed a genocide course and partnered programs and film presentations dealing with the Armenian Genocide.

Eva Hightaian (née Haroian)

Eva Haroian Hightaian in the U.S.

Eva married George Hightaian. She raised her own family while working alongside her husband, who had launched his own business, Lincoln Laundry. Eva was a member of the Armenian Apostolic Holy Trinity Church and its Women Auxiliary, and she was a founding member of its Mr. and

Mrs. Club. Eva was a longtime member of the Armenian Relief Society and a longtime advisor to the Armenian Youth Federation.

Eva Haroian Hightaian with her husband George

Eva Hightaian with her first-born child, Victor.

EVA HIGHTAIAN WITH HER INFANT SON VICTOR AND SAMUEL TOOMASIAN, WHO AS A
SEVEN-YEAR-OLD CHILD HAD WORKED THE FIELDS WITH GULEEG HAROIAN AFTER THE
1895 GREAT MASSACRES.

VICTOR HIGHTAIAN, OFFICER, W.W. II

The photographs below show the lifelong relationship among Guleeg
Haroian, Eva Hightaian (née Haroian), and the women involved in recording

their oral histories. For there was one more reason that so many histories of females and child survivors were lost. The main reasons given are the Turkish government's denial that led to an emphasis on Western testimonies; the Armenian community's taboo on females disclosing sexual trauma and forced marriages; and the lower literacy among females at that time and in that place. Some trained interviewers did attempt to record the histories of female survivors; however, these interviewers were professionals, meaning they were most often strangers to the female and child survivors and, equally important, these professional interviewers were most often men. The female survivors—if they consented at all to be interviewed— heavily edited their histories for these professional but unknown and largely male interviewers. The oral histories of Guleeg Haroian and Eva Hightaian, however, were delivered to the survivors' closest female relatives whom they trusted.

(Left to right): Eva Hightaian, Louise (daughter), and Rose in uniform

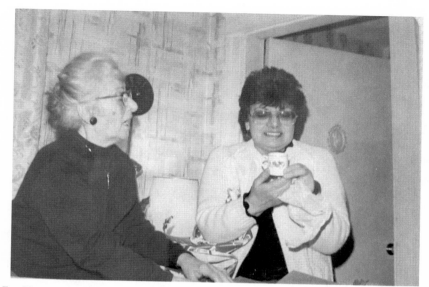

Eva Hightaian enjoying having her coffee grounds read by her younger sister Rose at Christmas.

Mary Tashjian unwrapping Christmas gift from niece Gil Harootunian. Mary Tashjian was responsible for ensuring Memoirs of a Soldier about the Days of Tragedy by Bedros Haroian was gifted to Gil Harootunian for editing and publishing.

THE NEXT GENERATION: (LEFT TO RIGHT): LOUISE (DAUGHTER OF EVA); EVA HIGHTAIAN; GIL HAROOTUNIAN (BRIDE); MARY TASHJIAN; AND ROSE GUERIN

References

Akçam, Taner. *Killing Orders: Talaat Pasha's Telegrams and the Armenian Genocide.* NY: Macmillan, 2018.

Armenian Immigration Project. "Search Military by Registration Location." URL: http://markarslan.org/ArmenianImmigrants/Public-ViewSummary-ArmenianImmigrants-Military-ByRegistrationLocation.php?SelectCountry=USA&SelectRegistrationStateProvince=MA&Staging=. Accessed 14 December 2022.

Atkinson, Tacy. *The German, the Turk and the Devil Made a Triple Alliance: Harpoot Diaries, 1908-1917.* Foreword by J. Michael Hagopian. Princeton, NJ: Gomidas Institute, 2000.

Balakian, Grigoris. *Armenian Golgotha: A Memoir of the Armenian Genocide, 1915-1918.* Trans. Peter Balakian and Aris Sevag. New York: Alfred A. Knopf, 2009.

Balakian, Peter. *The Burning Tigris: The Armenian Genocide and America's Response.* NY: HarperCollins, 2003.

Barton, James L., Compiler. *Turkish Atrocities: Statements of American Missionaries on the Destruction of Christian Communities in Ottoman Turkey, 1915-1917.* Ann Arbor, MI: Gomidas Institute, 1998.

Bedoukian, Kerop. *Some of Us Survived: The Story of an Armenian Boy.* NY: Farrar Straus Giroux, 1978.

Bilal, Melissa. "Lullabies and the Memory of Pain: Armenian Women's Remembrance of the Past in Turkey." *Dialectical Anthropology*. 43: 185-206. 2019. DOI 10.1007/s10624-018-9515-8.

Bjornlund, Matthias (2009). "'A Fate Worse Than Dying': Sexual Violence during the Armenian Genocide." In Herzog D. (ed.) *Brutality and Desire. Genders and Sexualities in History*. Palgrave Macmillan. London. DOI: 10.1057/9780230234291_2.

California State University, Fresno (September 1 – October 31, 2018). "Genocides of the 20th Century." Sponsored by Armenian Studies Program and Henry Madden Library, in cooperation with the Mémorial de la Shoah. Designed, created, and distributed by the Mémorial de la Shoah in Paris, France. In-person visit. Site: https://library.fresnostate.edu/content/genocides-exhibition-2018.

Dadrian, Vahakn. "Children as Victims of Genocide: The Armenian Case." *Journal of Genocide Research* (2003), 5(3), September, 421-437.

Darbinyan, Asya. "Recovering the Voices of Armenian Refugees in Transcaucasia: Accounts of Suffering and Survival." *Armenian Review*, 57 (1-2), 2020, 1 – 35.

Davis Leslie A. *American Consul in Harput (Mamouret-ul-Aziz), 1914 – 1917: Report No. 173, December 1915* in *Diplomats Witness and Condemn the Armenian Genocide: Collections of Documents and Testimonies*. Comp. and ed. Éva Merenics. Yerevan: National Academy of Sciences of the Republic of Armenia: Armenian Genocide Museum-Institute, 2016.

Davis, Leslie A. *The Slaughterhouse Province: An American Diplomat's Report on the Armenian Genocide, 1915-1917*. Ed. Susan K. Blair. New Rochelle, NY: Aristide D. Caratzas, Publisher, 1989.

Derderian, Katharine. "Common Fate, Different Experience: Gender-Specific Aspects of the Armenian Genocide, 1915-1917." *Holocaust and Genocide Studies*, 19(1): pages 1-25, spring 2005.

Der Hovhanessian, Diana. *About Time*. NY: Ashod Press: 1987.

Ekmekcioglu, Lerna. "A Climate for Abduction, a Climate for Redemption: The Politics of Inclusion during and after the Armenian Genocide." *Comparative Studies in Society and History*. 55(3): 522-553. 2013. DOI: 10.1017/S0010417513000236.

——. *Recovering Armenia: The Limits of Belonging in Post-Genocide Turkey*. CA: Stanford University Press, 2016.

Göçek, Fatma Müge. *Denial of Violence: Ottoman Past, Turkish Present, and Collective Violence against the Armenians: 1789-2009*. New York, NY: Oxford UP, 2015.

Greene, Frederick Davis and Henry Davenport Northrop. *Armenian Massacres: Or The Sword of Mohammed … Including a Full Account of the Turkish People*. Washington, D.C.: Office of the Librarian of Congress, 1896.

Haroian, Bedros. *Memoirs of a Soldier about the Days of Tragedy*. Published 1963. English translation. Fresno, CA: Tadem Press, 2021.

Harris, J. Rendel and Helen R. Harris. *Letters from the Scenes of the Recent Massacres in Armenia*. James Nisbet & Co., Ltd., London, 1897.

Hewsen, Robert. *Armenia: A Historical Atlas*. Chicago: University of Chicago Press, 2001.

Haroian, Guleeg. Personal Interview [follow up to "At Four O'Clock in the Afternoon." Oral history]. Trans. Rose D. Guerin. Edited Gil Harootunian. 1976.

Hightaian, Eva Haroian. Personal Interview [follow up to "Bones and Bodies, We Had To Walk Over Them." Oral history]. Edited Gil Harootunian. 1987.

Hoogasian-Villa, Susie and Mary Kilbourne Matossian. *Armenian Village Life Before 1914*. Detroit: Wayne State UP, 1982.

Jacobsen, Maria. *Diaries of a Danish Missionary: Harpoot, 1907-1919.* Trans. Kristen Vind. Ed. Ara Sarafian. Princeton, NJ: Gomidas Institute Books, 2001.

Jinks, Rebecca. "'And My Mother Gave Me Away': Armenian Women Survivors' Stories of Absorption and Reintegration During and After Genocide." California State University, Fresno Armenian Studies Lecture, September 15, 2022. Can be accessed at https://www.youtube.com/watch?v=GdkRKipCPCM.

Kaloosdian, Robert Aram. *Tadem: My Father's Village: Extinguished During the 1915 Armenian Genocide.* Peter E. Randall Publisher, Portsmouth, NH: 2015.

Kévorkian, Raymond. *The Armenian Genocide: A Compete History.* London: I.B. Tauris, 2011.

Khardalian, Suzanne. *Armenian Grandma's Tattoos Director: Comments after Viewing of the Film at St. Leon Armenian Church Center, New Jersey*: https://www.youtube.com/watch?v=9tM9pNYv8fQ Accessed 22 November 2022.

Khardalian, Suzanne. *Grandma's Tattoos: The Fate of Women During the Armenian Genocide.* Producer: PeÅ Holmquist This is the version aired on AL Jazeera *Witness* English 58 min, Sweden 2012. Accessed: https://www.academia.edu/video/1wwBw1?email_video_card=title&pls=RVP.

Kieser, Hans-Lukas. *Talaat Pasha: Father of Modern Turkey*, Architect of Genocide. NJ: Princeton UP, 2018.

Lepsius, Johannes. *Armenia and Europe: An Indictment.* Ed. J. Rendel Harris. London: Hodder and Stoughton, 1897. Retrieved from Google Books: https://books.google.com.

MacKeen, Dawn Anahid. *The Hundred Year Walk: An Armenian Odyssey.* NY: Mariner Books, 2016.

Manuk-Khaloyan, Armen. "'Rescued and Safe': Armenian Orphans and the Experience of Genocide." Center for Armenian Remembrance Occasional Paper. Retrieved from:

https://www.academia.edu/2425274/ Rescued and Safe Armenian Orphans and the Experience of Genocide Center for Armenian Rememberance Occasional Paper?email work card=view-paper.

Maksudyan, Nazan. "The Armenian Genocide and Survival Narrative of Children." *Childhood Vulnerability Journal* (1): 15-30. 2018. DOI: 10.1007/s41255-019-00002-8.

Marsden, Philip. *The Crossing Place: A Journey among the Armenians*. London: William Collins, 2015.

Mayersen, Deborah. "The 1895-1896 Armenian Massacres in Harput: Eyewitness Account." *The Massacres of the Hamidian Period (I): Global Narrative and Local Approaches*. 10, 2018, pages 161-183. DOI: https://doi.org/10.4000/eac.1641.

Miller, Donald E. and Lorna Touryan Miller. *Survivors: An Oral History of the Armenian Genocide*. University of California Press: Berkeley, CA: 1993.

Morgenthau, Henry. *Ambassador Morgenthau's Story: The Documented Account of the Armenian Genocide: First Genocide of the Century Reported by America's Ambassador to Turkey*. Plandome, NY: New Age Publishers, 1919.

Morris, Benny and Dror Ze'evi. *The Thirty-Year Genocide: Turkey's Destruction of Its Christian Minorities: 1894-1924*. Cambridge, MA: Harvard UP, 2019.

Mouradian, Khatchig, *The Resistance Network: The Armenian Genocide and Humanitarianism in Ottoman Syria, 1915-1918*. East Lansing, MI: Michigan State UP, 2021.

Northrop, Henry Davenport. *The Mohammedan Reign of Terror in Armenia*. Philadelphia and Chicago: International Publishing, Co. Entered according to an Act of Congress, in the year 1896, by J.R. Jones. Published by

Franklin Classics (imprint Creative Media Partners: support.creative-media.io).

Okkenhaug, Inger Marie. "Scandinavian Missionaries, Gender and Armenian Refugees during World War I: Crisis and Reshaping of Vocation." *Social Sciences and Mission* 23 (2010) 63-93. DOI 10.1163/187489410X488521.

Pattie, Susan Paul. *The Armenian Legionnaires: Sacrifice and Betrayal in World War I.* New York and London: I.B. Tauris, 2018.

Peroomian, Rubina. "Women and the Armenian Genocide: The Victim, the Living Martyr." *In Plight and Fate of Women During and Following Genocide.* Ed. Samuel Totten. Transaction Publishers. New Brunswick, NJ: 2009. Pages 7-24.

Pierce, Rev. James Wilson, D.D. *The Story of Turkey and Armenia*, and "A Sketch of Clara Barton and the Red Cross." Illus. Baltimore: R.H. Woodward Co., 1896.

Power, Samantha. *A Problem from Hell: America and the Age of Genocide.* NY: Basic Books: 2013.

Riggs, Henry H. *Days of Tragedy in Armenia: Personal Experiences in Harpoot, 1915-1917.* Ann Arbor, MI: Gomidas Institute, 1997.

Roberts, David. "Riddles of the Anasazi: toward the end of the 13th century, something went terribly wrong among the Anasazi. What awful event forced the people to flee their homeland, never to return?" *Smithsonian*, vol. 34, no. 4, July 2003, p. 72. *Gale Academic OneFile*, link. gale.com/apps/doc/A104997432/AONE?u=csufresno&sid=bookmark-AONE&xid=0a06a3fa. Accessed 7 Sept. 2022.

Rogan, Eugene. *The Fall of the Ottomans: The Great War in the Middle East.* New York: Basic Books, 2015.

Sanasarian, Eliz. "Gender Distinction in the Genocidal Process: A Preliminary Study of the Armenian Case." *Holocaust and Genocide Studies*, 4:4, 449-461, 1989. https://doi.org/10.1093/hgs/4.4.449.

Sarafian, Ara. "The Absorption of Armenian Women and Children into Muslim Households as a Structural Component of the Armenian Genocide." *In God's Name: Genocide and Religion in the Twentieth Century*, edited by Omer Bartov and Phylis Mac, 1st ed., Berghahn Books, 2010, pp. 209-21. JSTOR, http://www.jstor.org/stable/j.ctt9qcq8t.12. Accessed August 31, 2022.

Sarafian, Ara. *United States Official Documents on the Armenian Genocide. Volume III: The Central Lands.* Watertown, MA: Armenian Review, 1995.

Shipley, Alice Muggerditchian. *We Walked, Then Ran.* Mesa, AZ: Print Peddler, 1983.

Tachjian, Vahé. *Daily Life in the Abyss: Genocide Dairies, 1915-1918.* New York: Berghahn Books, 2019. Stable URL: Introduction from Daily Life in the Abyss: Genocide Diaries, 1915-1918 on JSTOR.

Tachjian, Vahé. "Gender, Nationalism, Exclusion: The Reintegration Process of Female Survivors of the Armenian Genocide." *Nations and Nationalism.* 15(1), pages 60-80, 2009.

Tashjian, Thomas. "Collection from the Old Country." Received by Gil Harootunian (editor), 31 December 2022.

Tashjian, Thomas. "Worcester Tornado Paragraph—Please Confirm Details." Received by Gil Harootunian (editor), 17 – 19 December 2022.

Walker, Christopher J. *Armenia: The Survival of a Nation.* NY: St. Martin's Press, 1980.

Watenpaugh, Keith David. "Are There Any Children for Sale?": *Genocide and the Transfer of Armenian Children (1915-1922). Journal of Human Rights*, 12:283-295, 2013. DOI:10.1080/14754835.2013.812410.

End Notes

1   Further research is needed into how these experiences were reflected in the Armenian culture, for example child rearing practices. MacKeen records the adage of her Armenian grandfather: "Men go through life walking on an unknown path. Every step must be taken in the dark" (2016, page 64). Rose D. Guerin (née Haroian) recalled similar child rearing practices of her father, Hagop Haroian, for example his compelling her to overcome her fear of the dark. Rose's nephew Thomas wrote that even his mother Mary (older sister of Rose) remembered vividly their father's tactic: Their "father wanted to make sure that his daughters were strong… Each night, knowing Rose was afraid of the dark, he would ask her to come to him, and then he would give her a cup and ask her to go out to the well and get him some cold water. [Rose] would point out the well inside by the sink but he would say it was better and colder from the well outside, and she would do it out of her great love for him." Thomas thought that was why Rose "*jarbig*… had no flies on her" (Tashjian, 17 - 19 December 2022).

2   Sources may exist in Armenian. I am referring to English language sources and all known translations into English of other sources.

3   To grasp how remote this region was, when two Red Cross teams arrived in Kharpert (the capital city of the province in which Tadem lay) after the 1894-1896 Great Massacres, these two teams became "… only the second group of non-missionary foreigners to visit the region in forty years" (Mayersen, page 10). The American Consul, Leslie

Davis, more than once stressed "… the peculiar conditions of this isolated region." After the 1915 Genocide, Davis toured the disturbingly emptied Armenian villages: "This country is isolation complete" (published in Sarafian, 1995, pages 3 and 144). The Reverend Pierce, a missionary in the late 1800s, describes the interior: "The roads are nothing but bridle-paths; they are infested with brigands, and there are no inns. Geographical isolation is not the least of the hardships in the present crisis" (page 13). In such isolation, Turkish or Kurdish aghas with the cruelest dispositions had free reign. One missionary observed: "Armenian prisoners are very often tortured; but a good deal depends upon the place. Some prisons are very bad, being noted for the abominable things that go on inside their walls; others are not so horrible. The prison of Erzeroum, for example, is not nearly so bad as that of Bitlis, though there, too, torture is occasionally employed in a fiendish way. The reason is, I conjecture, that the foreign consuls in Erzeroum can always get information about what goes on in the prison there, and the authorities are restrained by the knowledge of this" (Pierce, 1896, page 412; *see also* page 454).

4   Hightaian, Eva Haroian. "Bones and Bodies, We Had To Walk Over Them." Oral history. Ed. Gil Harootunian.

5   This role reversal also applied to single female Christian missionaries during the 1915 Genocide (*see* Okkenhaug, 2010). Okkenhaug's work discussed in-depth how these women risked their lives to form illegal relief networks and carried out both rescue work and publication of the Genocide despite strict Turkish censorship. The female missionaries also hid Armenian refugees and helped Armenians flee by disguising them as Kurds or Arabs.

6   U.S. Consul Davis notes that some from the towns had enough funds "to purchase their lives from the gendarmes who accompanied them but apparently all those from the villages were massacred. In the case of many of the large villages no word has been received from a single

person who was deported from them" (2016, page 154). The experiences of the Great Massacres also differed, based on the small size and isolation of villages. One missionary observed that several towns had successfully been able to resist massacre "but I cannot at present recall a successful defence of a village" (1897, page 148).

7   One might argue exceptions, such as the prisons in cities. For instance, Riggs in the main city of the Kharpert province notes: "Persons passing the prison at night reported hearing groans and shrieks coming from the victims" (1997, page 48). Kévorkian records that an official at the government accounting office who lived opposite the prison asked a German friend "to take him in for a few days because he could no longer bear the racket caused by the bastinadoes" (2011, page 410). However, hearing the agony of individual prisoners still would not allow a person in the city to grasp the scope of the horror.

8   Grigoris Balakian, a leading Armenian intellectual, who had experienced first-hand the horrors of the Genocide, arrived at the same counsel: "…I do not want to judge all of the other surviving Armenians. It was enough that they should save themselves any way they could" (2009, page 141).

9   The central government planned the deceit and out-of-sight butchery in the more populated towns and cities such as Yozgat. Talaat Pasha, Minister of Interior and the architect of the Genocide, issued explicit orders that "temporary implementation of compassionate treatment is necessary for political reasons" in cities, town, and other population centers, but that "the usual measures (massacres) known to you should be implemented in the appropriate regions" (Akçam, 2018, page 211; Morris and She'evi, 2019, pages 503-504).

10   U.S. Consul Leslie Davis was located in the main city, Mezre, of the province of Kharpert. In *The Slaughterhouse Province*, U.S. Consul Leslie Davis writes of his uncovering the ruse of 'deportations': "I wanted to investigate the fate of the people who had been sent away,

as it was said that many of them were killed only a short distance from the town, and I had made several trips without finding any trace of them. Finally, a Turk told me in strict confidence that he had seen thousands of dead bodies around Lake Goeljuk and offered to take me to the places where they were." U.S. Consul Leslie Davis soon discovers tens of thousands of bodies of 'deportees,' not only murdered but mutilated and robbed to nakedness (1989, pages 79-87). Not only did this horrify Consul Davis, but also some Ottoman citizens would have been horrified. In *Armenia: A Historical Atlas*, Robert H. Hewsen notes that the "outright massacre" of the Armenian women and children "might horrify local public opinion and even alienate the Muslim clergy" so 'deportations' were devised as a means to exterminate the Armenians out of sight (page 233).

11   See Mouradian (2021) for a study of the numerous informal and unarmed civilian resistance networks that operated during and post-Genocide. Mouradian notes that women were central forces in these resistance networks and to focus only on the 'warrior element' of resistance diminishes "the importance of women's contributions" (page xvii). Kévorkian notes networks of women or with women participants, including one in Constantinople: "It is noteworthy that young women ensured the network's communications and transported weapons earmarked for the banned activists" (2011, pages 539-540).

12   Khanum Kilivchan despised her husband Hadji Bego and his sons and grandsons, and she, too, formed a spontaneous local underground railroad with her brother who came at night and took Armenians to his Kurdish village, Khamishlu (Haroian, Bedros, 2021, page 177).

13   Anna leverages her network later to save her husband, Bedros Haroian, who had escaped from his Ottoman Army labor battalion and imminent death (Haroian, 2021, 178-185).

14   The *Memoirs of a Soldier about the Days of Tragedy* confirms that Yeva was under the protection of Yousouph *agha* (Haroian, 2021, page 178).

15   Guleeg states that she is sheltering with his "sister," Bado Haroian (Bedros Haroian, 2021, pages 112, 178, 181, 182, 183) though Bado is an in-law. In these circumstances, Armenians typically made other Armenians their primary relatives (sister, brother).

16   Another example shows the skill of Armenian women in brokering marriages. Levon Harootunian was the grandfather of Sarkis Harootunian, the cartographer for this book. Levon was serving in the U.S. Army in W.W. I when he was wounded. He was recuperating in a hospital in France when he learned of an Armenian refugee camp. Levon took the bus there, met, and eventually proposed to Vartouhi Karagulian. When Levon asked Vartouhi to marry him, her response was, "I have one sister and four cousins." He countered, "I am not a rich man, but I will see what I can do." Levon Harootunian and Vartouhi Karagulian married, and soon Levon's younger brother Sarkis Harootunian was corresponding with one of Vartouhi's cousins (Aghavni). A second marriage took place, and more followed.

17   Ekmekcioglu distinguishes between the specific actions and the alleged intentions behind those specific actions in accounts by Genocide survivors: "Given the mediated and after-the-fact nature of these and many other such accounts, we cannot assume authenticity. But for our purposes, the original intentions do not matter. What matters is how those acts were talked about and given meaning in the immediate post-war years." In other words, the women may allege a heroic intention behind an action (such as handing over a child to non-Armenians) while the actual intention may have been far less heroic. Yet, the study of the survivors' accounts reveals a common vocabulary that emerged, centered on restoring the nation and on taking revenge (2016, page 30). Maksudyan (2019) similarly notes child survivors "turn memories into adventures and the narrator into a hero" (page 16).

18   Okkenhaug's work shows Scandinavian female missionaries who formed illegal rescue networks also leveraged every ounce of

matriarchal authority they had (2010). These missionaries were called "Mother" by Armenians, and "The Mother title and role of Scandinavian female missionaries could thus be seen as a maternal equivalent of the Armenian patriarch, who also had responsibility for issues that concerned the material state of the community" (page 90). Moreover, Okkenhaug's work parallels Eva Hightaian's description of her mother as head of household. Okkenhaug writes: "While the single women missionaries were perceived of as 'mothers' for the orphans, the financial (and spiritual) supporters in Denmark were called "fathers." According to Karekin Dickran ... the donors – a group that to a large extent consisted of women – were seen as male. They were the breadwinners, i.e., the supporters of the home, which was traditionally a male duty" (page 92).

19 Women had two assets—gold and prettiness—and both were double-edged, making the women as liable to robbery and rape as to survival. Women like Guleeg Haroian were careful to hide both and deploy them skillfully. One statement sums it up with clarity: a Kurdish lord complied with government orders to kill the Armenians but noted that "he was saving pretty girls and those who had money" (Atkinson, 2000, page 48).

20 Guleeg has another asset: after years alone, working the fields and running the house, Guleeg was physically fit. Walker (1980) comments on the Death Marches, "Many of the deportees remained obstinately alive; a number were fit enough to withstand the wide differences of climate, from the Mediterranean type climate of Anatolia to the Arabian-type desert of north Syria, and the appalling privations of the journey" (page 226).

21 The Turkish name for Mezre in the Ottoman Empire was Mamuret-ul-Aziz. The modern Turkish name is Elazığ.

22 The *sofkeeat* was the collection, followed by immediate deportation. There is no direct transliteration from Armenian, (or, in this case,

Armenians using a Turkish word), and "sofkeeat" (phonetic rendering) is often written as *sevkiat* in American texts. However, Alice Shipley (née Muggerditchian), a survivor from the same province as Guleeg Haroian, spells the word "sofkiat" in her memoirs (1983, page 67).

23   One scholar provides a caution about labelling the survivors' actions "choices" – "Such are the tragic moral choices that genocide so often requires, although it is perhaps an overstatement to call them "choices." In these circumstances, people respond rather instinctively to what seems best given the requirements of the moment" (Miller and Miller, 1983, pages 97-98).

24   Balakian notes that even the most educated did not grasp initially the extent of the danger because "in human history from prehistoric times, there had never been a forced displacement of an entire nationality" (Balakian, Grigoris, 2009, page 24). Accounts from foreign witnesses confirm this. U.S. Consul Leslie Davis writes, "Although the difficulties of the journey were known to some extent, no one fully realized at that time what deportations really meant" (1989, page 58). Microhistories of survivors confirm this, for example: "They did sürgün [exile]. I don't know what it is" (Bilal, 2019, page 196). Scholars confirm this; for example, Mouradian's work on informal resistance networks notes that initially those organizers did not expect the flood of deportees whose situation would worsen without end (2021, page 5). Finally, *see* Kévorkian: "According to one survivor's report, while the Armenians feared a massacre like the one that had occurred in 1895, it occurred to none of them in this period that the government would this time implement a program of an entirely different scope and kind" (2011, pages 613-614). Kaloosdian applies this directly to Tadem: "Many Armenians could not imagine that a government would methodically destroy an entire population" (2015, page 79). In *Memoirs of a Soldier about the Days of Tragedy*, Bedros Haroian thinks similarly. He notes both the bravery of his fellow Armenian soldiers on the Caucasian front and the incompetent leadership of Enver Pasha that led to the

171

destruction of the Third Army on that front (2021, pages 128-146). The Young Turks leadership makes the Armenians soldiers scapegoats for its own failures and relegates the Armenians to labor battalions— against their Turkish Commander's wishes. Haroian writes, "Upon saying goodbye to our Commander, we went on the road with semi-happy thoughts and feelings. We believed we were going to be working on building roads, which wasn't going to be as bad as being on the front lines, especially in harsh winter conditions" (2021, page 149). That feeling rapidly evaporates as Haroian realizes the labor battalions are being worked to the point of death, and then slaughtered (Haroian, Bedros, 2021, page 392). See also Kévorkian, 2011, pages 240-242.

25   Australian scholar Keiser makes repeated mention of Talaat's note-books, for example: "Talaat was becoming a pioneering demographic engineer, as his notebook, with his fastidious statistical accounting testifies" (2018, page 13). Talaat's notebooks not only recorded demographics of deportees but also of their goods and properties looted: "Talaat noted in his pocketbook around late 1916 a part of the spoils: more than 40,000 buildings, 90,000 *dönüm* farmland (a *dönüm* is an Ottoman measurement of little more than 1,000 square meters [1,094 square yards]), and 26 mining concessions" (2018, page 268). Survivor testimonies confirm that exact counting of Armenians, even after the deportees were herded in the Deir Zor death camp: "A month ago, they took a census; they recorded where we come from how many we are" (MacKeen, 2016, pages 159-160). An example can illustrate the fastidiousness of Talaat's counting: "According to Talât's book-keeping, before the war there were 44,661 Armenians in the vilayet [Ankara]. After, there were 12,766, with 4,560 of Ankara's Armenians living in other vilayets" (Morris and Ze'evi, 2019, page 222). Talât demands statistics from local officials. As one instance, Sabit Bey, the Vali of Kharpert (the province in which Tadem lay) cabled Talât on 18 September 1915 a "balance sheet of the operations conducted in his region. He estimated the number of deported Armenians at 51,000;

4,000, he thought, were still hiding in the villages." Subsequently, "to find these fugitives and flush them out of their hiding places…. Vali Sabit needed to restore a climate of relative confidence." Vali Sabit Bey assured everyone that the last deportations were now over. Then, in November, remaining Armenians were flushed out and dispatched (Kévorkian, 2011, pages 400-401; Davis, 2016, pages 150 and 151-152; *see also* Kaloosdian, 2015, pages 123-131). Danish missionary Jacobsen in Mezre observed, "The soldiers are now going from house to house making note of the number of people, and telling them when they are to be ready to leave on exile" (2001, page 75). In a missionary hospital, one Armenian soldier in "delirium kept saying, 'Count the Armenians, count the Armenians'" before he succeeded in killing himself (Atkinson, 2000, page 80). The Young Turks were perfecting the aim of the 1894-1896 Great Massacres to "alter the proportion of Christians to Mohammedans" in the six Eastern provinces that had numerous Armenians (Greene and Northrop, 1896, page 40).

26   The *vorpahavak* reclaimed both children and brides because "women without a male relative were also considered orphans" in the patriarchal Armenian society of that era (Ekmekcioglu, 2016, page 28).

27   Toros' decision to run away would have been 'wise' based on his experience. Many Armenians who survived did so by constant and repeated escaping of the collections. For a summary analysis of the Turkish methods of slaughtering child survivors, see Dadrian (2003): the child survivors were collected and killed by three primary methods: drowning operations, burning alive, and wholesale rapes of the girls and the boys, after which they were systemically murdered. The burning alive and other tortures of children could take place in front of large crowds and Turkish notables to impress them with the urgent need to erase the Armenians from the Ottoman Empire. *See also* Mouradian, 2021, pages 136-138.

28 I use "lawless" in the sense of the non-romanticized Wild West of the U.S.

29 Mardin, though in Turkey, was a city populated by Syrians (until post-WW I), so the Armenians referred to that city and the region as "Syria."

30 Guleeg's stage in life should also be taken into account: she is senior now, and her husband Hagop has died decades before from bacterial pneumonia.

31 Illiteracy was widespread at that time, so sworn testimonies were the norm.

32 Eva Haroian Hightaian clarifies these young women were later married to Armenian men in Cilicia, a territory under Allied [French] protection at the time and where many Armenian refugees had gathered or been gathered (for safety) (Hightaian, Personal Interview).

33 Guleeg Haroian was born with another first name, but when she was one-year old, an infant named Guleeg died, and she was re-christened with that baby's name. Guleeg Haroian stated that naming a baby after a friend or relative who had just died "was a custom" in the village (Haroian, Personal Interview). Hoogasian-Villa, working with Armenian-American respondents to document Armenian village life before 1914, mentions the custom of naming children after a living person, thought to increase the lifespan of the individual and perpetuate his or her name (1982, page 106). The practice of naming a child after a recently deceased person would also perpetuate the name.

34 The name "Haroian" also illustrates naming practices in the villages. Guleeg Haroian had married Hagop Haroian, whose maternal grandmother had been married to a Goshgarian, who died. The grandmother had one boy. In her oral history, Eva Hightaian (née Haroian) clarified that John [Ovan] Haroian married the Goshgarian widow, but he said, "I don't want your little boy to be Goshgarian because I have no children. I want to adopt him." Ovan Haroian adopted him

so the little boy would perpetuate the Haroian name and have inheritance rights.

35   German Pastor Johannes Lepsius gives an overview specific to Tadem: "… came to Tadem. Here we rode up a high hill which commands the village, and the whole scene of devastation lay before us. Formerly the village contained 250 houses, of which 200 are now blackened heaps of ruins. The only lot of timber which we saw lay near the house of the Agas, who, by means of forced labour, were building a magnificent 'konak' [government house]" (1897, pages 125-126). Kaloosdian notes, "The only Armenian houses left standing were those that adjoined the homes of the Turks" (205, page 25). Also noted is the brutality of the murders of Armenians: "The dead were mutilated in the most cruel ways imaginable. Axes, meat-cleavers, etc., were used. Those killed by firearms are considered as the happiest ones" (missionary cited in Mayersen, 2018, page 9). Lepsius provides a summary of the combined factors of the Great Massacres. He notes able-bodied men were killed; harvests and livestock stolen; homes and churches plundered then set on fire; many Armenians forced to convert to Islam; and the destitute surviving Armenians who remained Christian were abandoned to their fate (often, a slow death). The result is "…a famine of the most gigantic proportions was reigning in Armenia … and is still reigning, and that 500,000 men, in order to escape death by starvation, are in actual fact dependent on the support of the Christians of the West" (1897, page 118; see also pages 122 and 270-271). Harris notes the Kurds and Turks returned to some villages "to plunder them of the oxen purchased for them by some of the relief workers" (1897, page 148).

36   *Agha* is a Turkish title for chief; local overlord.

37   The currency was gold, so "our wealth was taken to his house" means Mamood *agha* carted away the gold. Women could wear ornamental gold jewelry to make visible family status, but mostly Armenians hid

their wealth due to chronic massacres, daily abuses, and the general lack of security in the Ottoman Empire. That is why Guleeg Haroian's father had to reveal where the whereabouts of that gold to Mamood *agha*, who then shot Guleeg's Haroian father once he knew the hiding place of the family gold. Eva Hightaian (née Haroian) elaborated that her grandfather George Toomasian had clay pots filled with gold pieces hidden in the sunken storage kitchen. She stated that when the killing began, the wild and hungry Kurds from the mountains spent hours taking the clay pots of gold hidden in the pantry and all family possessions. German pastor Lepsius observes that the local governors were careful to get their cut: "In Harpout the *Vali*, Mustafa *pasha*, secured to himself a portion of the booty by drawing a cordon of Circassians round the city, and any especially valuable articles which were being carried away he ordered to be seized and set aside for himself" (1897, page 57).

38   Father Aharon Aharonian. Father Aharon was Guleeg's maternal uncle. He was murdered and flayed along with at least a dozen other priests in the region. German Pastor Johannes Lepsius identifies my grandmother's uncle, Father Aharon, among the priests who were "skinned" (1897, pages 26 and 270). Flaying was a common form of torture (Derderian, 2005, pages 367, 444, 459). Priests not flayed were often tortured by having body parts chopped off before being murdered (page 39). Lepsius provides more details on the atrocities that took place in the province of Kharpert, singling out Tadem: "The baker in Kesserik who had already murdered ninety-seven Armenians, which he proved by exhibiting their ears and noses, declared that he would not rest till he had brought up the number to 100. But he found his master in Hadji Begos of Tadem, who had butchered more than 100 Christians, and who, as a sign of his prowess, cut a woman in four pieces and put them on the posts to public view" (page 23) and "hunted a Christian girl naked through the streets" (page 28). Hadji Bego of Tadem was monstrous to the point he survives in the

literature today as an example of a raging mass murderer and mass rapist (Morris and Ze'evi, 2019, page 123; Kaloosdian, 2015, pages 23-30).

39 Bedros Haroian names the murderers in *Memoirs of a Soldier About the Days of Tragedy*: "Tosun *agha* had two brothers—Shikrin and Mahmut—who were brutal and cold-hearted. They dragged the priest Aharon Aharonian out of his house and stabbed him. Father Aharon, wounded, hid in the gardens, and escaped to Aghunkar at night. But the Turkish peasants of Yelnizkoy village spied him and killed him, and then burned his body.... Father Aharon's brother, who had come from Mezre, secretly watched what was going on, but he could not do anything to help his brave brother. With grief in his heart, he returned to Mezre and died after fifteen days." (page 16). Kaloosdian identifies "Ovsanna Der Vartanian's father" as the man who tried to carry Father Aharon to Aghunkar (2015, page 24).

40 The silence of Guleeg Haroian on the fate of her grandmother is similar to a director slamming down the top board and yelling, "Cut!" The screen goes blank: the scene is cut. We learn from Kaloosdian that Guleeg Haroian's grandmother was murdered by being thrown "down a wheat well" (2015, page 23). Scholarship on the Great Massacres amply documents the mass gang rapes and abduction of both women and children. After her uncle is dragged out and shot, Guleeg speaks not of the fate of the women left behind. To Guleeg, in that time and place, that fate of those women was unspeakable. One testimonial on the fate of women in Tadem during the Great Massacres estimated that about 350 out of Tadem's approximate 1,000 women had been raped (Morris and She'evi, 2021, page 123). Lepsius describes the savagery: "The valour of the populace and soldiery was not checked by any thought of risk to their own lives. They could give full rein to their delight in the massacres and the orgies which followed them" (1897, pages 21, 28-29). Lepsius continues to describe how the women are "...outraged with such accompaniments of nameless brutality that

their agonies often culminate in a horrible death. Girls of eleven and twelve—nay, of nine—are torn from their families and outraged in this way by a band of 'men' whose names are known, and whose deeds are approved by the representative of law and order" (1897, page 248; *see also* Pierce, 1896, page 423). Greene and Northrop note, "Little girls of five and six were frequently forced to be present during these horrible scenes of lust, and, they, too, were often sacrificed before the eyes of their mothers" (1896, page 326). Morris and She'evi similarly note the rapes of "women and girls" (aged 12-40) (2021, page 92).

41   Missionaries helped to reclaim women and children who had been abducted during the Great Massacres. One provides a description of the magnitude of the task: "…there are the poor ruined village girls who have been brought back, after months of imprisonment worse than death, from Kurdish homes, recovered at last by the indefatigable efforts of the French and English Consuls. There are many of these now in Diarbekir who have no homes and no parents to return to, and whose moral nature as well as physical health is all crushed and broken with what they have gone through. Again, what is to be done with them? I have told my small committee to try and find them *some* work—*anything* to occupy their minds—and to feed and clothe them (Harris, 1897, page 131). J. Rendel Harris similarly writes "the needs are unspeakable" in *Letters from the Scenes of the Recent Massacres in Armenia* (1897, page 10). Moreover, the missionaries had to decline the demands of the Turks in Harpoot who barred the missionaries' relief efforts and proposed the money be given directly to them (the Turks) (page 19).

42   One missionary observed not only had all the men been taken, but also the "strongest and ablest and wisest," so that in families "perhaps only the grandfather with a handful of children" was left (1897, page 62).

43   The fates of Samuel and Mampreh Toomasian differed. Mampreh Toomasian like many other young Armenian men in America left to join the Armenian volunteers fighting in the Armenian Legion or on the Caucasian front. Mampreh Toomasian died on the battle-field on the Caucasian front (Haroian, 2021, pages 307-308). Samuel Toomasian (b. March 1887 in Tadem) immigrated to America and registered for the draft in the U.S. on June 5, 1917. He survived and flourished (*see* photograph in "Editor's Note: A Legacy of Good" at the end of this volume).

44   The "Armenian Immigration Project" hints at the flow of young men out of Tadem after the 1895 Great Massacre. The "Armenian Immigration Project" identifies 60 young men from Tadem who regis-tered for the draft for W.W. I in the United States. The actual numbers of young men from Tadem in the U.S. would be much higher because those 60 includes only those who self-reported down to the village level (Tadem) and not the many who only reported at the country (Turkey) or at the country plus province (Kharpert). Moreover, fear and danger were so high that families sent boys who were only 14 or 15 to the U.S. (listing their ages as 16 or above), and these boys once in the U.S. would not have been old enough to register for the draft. A good number of older Armenian boys or young men also escaped to Russia, a shorter and less expensive route, and one that led to the thriving Armenian community in Tbilisi and other cities. A formal collection and study of this data would be of interest to the field of Armenian Genocide studies, for it could confirm the extent to which the 1915 Armenian Genocide killed the old men, women, and children left in the villages. Finally, the few young men remaining in Tadem at the outbreak of W.W. I were drafted into the Ottoman Army in 1914.

45   Elizabeth was named after her paternal grandmother, Elizabeth Haroian (née Mentsoian), and also the name of one of Hagop Haroian's sisters. Hagop Haroian had three sisters. The oldest Mariam married into the Narzhonts (Najarian) family. The youngest, Margaret, married

into the Vanetzian family. The third sister (who must be this Elizabeth) married into the Nordigian family.

46   The baby George died in 1914, a harsh and war-ridden year. In the spring, locusts overran the fields and orchards; in the fall, the government requisitioned 20 bushels of wheat to feed the soldiers along with horses and oxen; livestock disease became widespread; the government conscripted the men, and the government closed all exit routes under martial law (Kaloosdian, pages 51-56).

47   Guleeg Haroian uses two terms for the 1915 Genocide: *Aksor* and *Medz Chart*, the latter term commonly used in Anatolia, the eastern region of Turkey where the village of Tadem lay (see for example Bilal, 2018, pages 192-193).

48   Prior to modern reforms, Armenians were barred from entering the military. The prohibition was then used to deride them compared to the Muslim population who were skilled in the use of firearms and horseback riding (Göçek, 2015, page 132). Greene described the Armenians in the Ottoman Empire: "…few in number, scattered and unarmed" (1896, page 179). In the eastern provinces, the Kurds were "armed to the teeth" (Kévorkian, 2011, pages 151-152). Moreover, the Sultan had armed the Kurdish irregulars. Hagop Haroian's insight that he will be given trouble as an Armenian in the Ottoman Army will prove both prophetic and a gross understatement. When the Genocide commenced, the Armenian conscripts in the Ottoman Army were disarmed, worked to exhaustion in labor battalions, and then slaughtered. For a summary, see Footnote 111, "Murders of Armenian Soldiers in Ottoman Army" (Haroian, Bedros, 2021, page 392).

49   Herein lies a challenge with oral histories. Guleeg makes frequent references to "that region's Effendi" or "that Effendi" because she is addressing my mother and myself, and she knows that we have never been to Tadem, long wiped out as an Armenian village, and have no

knowledge of the characters she is mentioning. She uses the title, *Effendi*, to convey to us that this was a Turk with power in the village.

50   "Toomas" refers to the clan that Guleeg was from: the patriarch was Toomas (Thomas), and so those born to him bore the name of Toomasian. Guleeg was from the "House of Toomas" not unlike the "House of Montague" or "House of Capulet." She was referred to as "Toomas" the way someone might be referred to as a "Capulet" or "Montague."

51   The U.S. Commerce Department "Manifest of Alien Passengers" lists "Hagop Haroian" on the S.S. Oceanic sailing from Cherbourg, France on 28 May 1913. He arrived in Ellis Island on June 6, 1913.

52   On 31 October 1914, the Ottoman Empire formally entered WWI; the government instituted martial law.

53   When the war broke out, funds sent by Armenians in America were embargoed by the Turks, "never to be returned. The wealth of the Armenians was stolen yet again—this time the hard-earned money from America" (Kaloosdian, 2015, page 35).

54   Guleeg's use of the phrase "Turkish officials" includes all local Ottoman officials, many of whom in the Eastern provinces were Kurdish. The Armenian word "Turke" was "a common way of referring to Ottoman Muslims" (Ekmekcioglu, 2016, page 12).

55   Hadji Bego, an *agha* of Kurdish descent, arrived in Tadem shortly before the 1895 Great Massacres. Hadji Bego, his sons, and his associates (i.e., Kurdish gangsters) led the Great Massacres. Hadji Bego had four sons – Hafiz, Ibosh, Ahmed, and Moheiddin. Guleeg Haroian is identifying Hadji Bego's son Hafiz in this passage, who was now the governmental overseer of Tadem (his father Hadji Bego having died). Another of Hadji Bego's sons, Ibosh, had four sons, two of whom—Bekir and Ashreff—distinguished themselves in the murder and looting of Armenians and their homes in 1915.

56   Before the 1908 revolution, Armenian men could not bear arms, but they were allowed to wear a sword on their wedding day to fight against the widespread stealing and raping of young Armenian brides by Turks and Kurds. Eva Hightaian mentions this sword was green, white, and red, and these colors suggest this may be a wedding day sword (draped with red, green, and white ribbons). A crown made of red, green, and white threads was placed on the heads of the bride and groom, with green signifying life, red signifying sacrifice, and white signifying peace. Grooms also wore embroidered sashes of red and green pinned to white shirts.

57   Anna Sahagian married Bedros Haroian, the younger brother of Hagop. The Turkish Army had conscripted Bedros Haroian, but he escaped, and he survived to write *Memoirs of a Soldier about the Days of Tragedy*.

58   The "Turk" was, again, Hafiz, the Kurdish governmental overseer of Tadem and the son of Hadji Bego. Kaloosdian provides details on the torture (pages 76-77) as does Bedros Haroian in his *Memoirs*. U.S. Consul to Kharpert, Leslie Davis, uses "konak" to describe a Turkish palace in the city of Mezre in Kharpert (1989, page 60) though in the villages the "konak" would be the house of the *agha*.

59   In general, the "monstrous deformities" of persons who survived Ottoman torture bear witness to their ordeals (Pierce, 1896, page 408). Harris expressed his indignation at both the atrocities and the Turkish denial of atrocities: "Do they want me to bring home a collection of people with slashed heads and faces and minus hands and ears? Or to dig up the burnt bones from the caves and trenches into which they have been thrown by the sackful?" (1897, page 155). Shipley gives graphic details on the torture throughout her memoir but especially in chapter 11, "Atrocities" (1983, pages 56-58). Riggs describes the conditions of a few survivors brought in from the sites of massacres along the Death March: "...Some of those brought in were too horribly

mangled to recover …. Two little children whom the Kurds had started to behead were brought in, and the ghastly gashes across the backs of those two little necks were being treated while I was in the room. Other horrible wounds I will not describe" (1997, page 52). The list of examples of savage tortures discussed in the research on the Genocide makes it impossible to be inclusive here.

60　　Not only did military cordons prevent Armenians from receiving information, but all communication was strictly censored and, in remote regions, limited to town criers. This allowed the government to persist—initially—in lies to its Armenian citizens: "To appreciate the state of mind of the Armenians who were about to be deported, we must take an important factor into consideration: they were absolutely ignorant of the crimes being committed in other provinces" (Kévorkian, 2011, page 392).

61　　Mezre was the administrative center of the province, and the title of Vali (pronounced *val-lee*) means governor. The wagoneer in-law was Harootiun Altounian, whose daughter Pilazoon has married Boghos Haroian, the older brother of Hagop Haroian.

62　　The *Vali*, Sabit Bey, was Sabit Cemal Sağirzade (alternately Sağiroğlu with the Turkish suffix "oğlu" for "son of" Sağir). *Vali* Sabit Bey became notorious for his duplicity with the Armenians in his governance, for wholesale thieving of Armenian property, and for the murder of hundreds of thousands of deportees passing through his province. American missionary Henry Riggs writes, "He was responsible for the miserable suffering or death not only of the vast majority of the Armenians in his own province, but also of scores of thousands of Armenians from northern provinces, who were relatively safe till they entered his province, but within his jurisdiction were massacred wholesale or done to death in ways more cruel than out and out massacre" (Riggs, 1997, pages 77, 81-82, 83, 93). A Danish missionary observes, "Everybody says that although they had trouble and great danger on the way, the most terrible suffering started when they came to the Mezre vilayet. Now the soldiers are worse than animals. All the men they can lay their hands on are being literally slaughtered, the women ravished and beaten with thick sticks" (2001, page 77). When Sabit Bey promised to retrieve some friends of the missionaries who had been rounded up and deported if he received a telegram responding to the several telegrams of U.S. Consul Leslie Davis, the missionaries suspected "it is he who has held back the Consul's telegrams" (2001, page 97; *see also* Davis, 2016, page 150 on the interception of his reports). One official who had resisted the deportations noted that Sabit Bey was an "energetic partner" to the Young Turks in the deportations: "Sabit seemed in fact to relish the job, sending out joking, sarcastic telegrams about his victims" (Morris and She'evi, 2019, pages 190-192). Sabit Bey "unleashed a campaign" against Armenian leaders, including torturing Armenians and being strongly suspected of planting bombs on them to justify their treatment and sending photographs of his "war trophies" to Constantinople. He energetically organized "squadrons of *çetes* for the Special Organization," the criminals released from jail to kill the Armenians en route (Kévorkian, 2011, pages 384-387). When the American consul and missionaries paid Sabit Bey a visit shortly before the deportations began to ask him to show "mercy" and to allow them to accompany the Armenians on the difficult journey, he refused and proceeded to blame the Armenians for their fate, including citing the bombs he himself was suspected of planting on them (Kévorkian, 2011, page 389). Sabit Bey simultaneously made strenuous efforts to protect himself from being held accountable for his role in the Genocide (Morris and She'evi, 2019, pages 197-198). The U.S. Consul to the province, Leslie Davis, found Sabit Bey to be an "exceedingly ignorant and uncultured man ... gross in his manner," but "of considerable natural shrewdness" (1989, pages 40-41) who only obtained the post of Vali from the social standing of his feudal family (Kévorkian, 2011, page 283). Born in 1881, he lived a long life, dying in 1960. When the Allies became victorious in World War I, the British made a sincere attempt, initially, to hold accountable those officials responsible for the Genocide. Documentation included Sabit Bey's correspondence directing local officials to hide evidence that the deportations were genocidal by burying the "corpses strewn along the roads," and he increased his efforts upon admonition from Talât Pasha, Minister of the Interior (Kévorkian, 2011, page 424). The British imprisoned Sabit Bey at Malta along with other Ottoman officials (Kévorkian, 2011, page 792), until he was released as a result of negotiations, and—like many perpetrators of the genocide—rewarded with a high-ranking post by Mustafa Kemal Atatürk, the new President of Turkey (Kévorkian, 2011, pages 804-805). U.S. Consul Leslie Davis on site in the province during the Genocide provides a detailed portrait of the unstable character of Sabit Bey (1989, pages 40-42).

63 Scholars discuss how women whose male relatives were suspected of resistance experienced severe treatment to "intimidate Armenian leadership and dampen its will to resist" (Derderian, 2005, pages 5 - 6). Diana Der Hovhanessian describes the torture of her grandmother, Zarif, when she refused to reveal the hiding place of her son, a Dashnak youth who resisted oppressive rule (*About Time*, 1987, pages 24-25). The Turks smashed her right arm, flayed it, and then chopped it off. Chopping off the right hand or arm was a favorite form of torture in the Great Massacres also because it rendered the victims helpless their entire lives (Harris, 1897, pages 26, 116, 151). Harris offers an illustration: "One man was a coppersmith, but his hand was cut off; what could he do?" (1897, pages 60-61). Eyes were also gouged out to render the victims' helpless if they survived (Harris, 1897, page 32). Riggs notes that men who displayed courage or resistance were also subject to savagery, with the dead bodies being almost unrecognizable (1997, pages 53-54). Moreover, "The Turks always kept a watch on a family that had a demonstrated record of bravery and the first thing they did was to shoot them" (Kaloosdian, 2015, page 13). The wives

of the brave "Haroian brothers" were targets upon whom the Turks would have inflicted the worst treatment.

64   This brother-in-law was the husband of Takouhi, Guleeg's sister. The brother-in-law did not survive. After the war, Guleeg and Hagop Haroian helped Takouhi to immigrate to France and, eventually, re-marry there.

65   Ashreff was the grandson of Hadji Bego. Ashreff's father was Ibosh, one of the four sons of Hadji Bego.

66   Samantha Power, former U.S. ambassador to the United Nations, wrote *A Problem from Hell: America and the Age of Genocide*. She notes that Henry Morgenthau, the U.S. Ambassador to Turkey in 1915, raised money to transport Armenian survivors to the U.S., but "the Turks, insincere even about helping Armenians leave, blocked the exit of refugees. Morgenthau's plan went nowhere" (2013, page 12). Morgenthau's agreement with the Sublime Porte to exempt "naturalized Americans from deportation" was ignored (Kévorkian, 2011, page 390). Leslie Davis, the American Consul stationed in the region, clarifies in his report: "…although in some cases I presented passports or other documents, the result was that all persons of Armenian origin—those holding valid passports, those born in America, and all others—were refused permission to leave" (published in Sarafian, 1995, page 125; see also pages 131-132). Morris and She'evi notes that "Armenians were routinely prevented from leaving the empire, forced to stay and be killed" (2019, page 215).

67   The hourly coordination of the 1894-1896 Great Massacres as well as the hourly coordination of the 1915 Genocide indicate how methodical the Turks were in implementation. German pastor Johannes Lepsius noted the clocking of hours when reporting on the 1894-1895 Great Massacres: "The Turkish country-people spoke quite openly upon the subject: the Mullahs had said in the mosques that the Sheikh-ul-Islam, the spiritual chief of the Mohammedan world, has ordered

the extermination of the Armenians. As the authorities, at least in the towns, had only set apart a limited space of several hours or days for the massacres and pillage, and then had called a halt, there was only one feature of the whole matter obscure to the Turkish population. They could not understand why the life of a single Armenian was spared" (1897, pages xiii–xiv). Another on-site missionary, Reverend Pierce, confirms the "very day and hour were openly talked about" (1896, page 482), and goes on to state: "Killing goes on, say from ten to four, when the level [of killing] is supposed to be reached, but woe to a Turk who kills after four; he himself is summarily shot." Pierce gives the hours of 10 a.m. to 4 p.m. because his sources informed him the Turks were told, "Sharpen your swords; today you are to kill Armenians wherever you find them for six hours; after that you are to stop; and the blood of any Armenian you kill after this is my blood" (1896, pages 21, 92). Harris notes that the government ordered all shops opened and business was to be resumed as usual, and then "About noon a single shot was fired, and the slaughter immediately begun" (1897, page 210). Kévorkian in his analysis of the 1915 Genocide observed, "In the Ottoman Empire, massacres always began in the market, since the attackers were tempted by the goods that they could loot there" (2011, page 88). In Trebizond, one observer wrote, "Suddenly like a clap of thunder in a clear sky, the assault began at about 11 a.m. yesterday" (Greene and Northrop, 1896, page 310). In Erzerum, "The attack was made by Moslems after leaving the mosques, after the noon hour of prayer, and it was simultaneous all over the city" (Greene and Northrop, 1896, page 34). In Marsovan, the killing began after the noonday prayer and continued until four o'clock, when "the governor of the city walked through the streets of the market with a cane under his arm and said, for substance, "Now boys, you have done enough. Go home and behave yourselves. Don't let me hear of your making any more disturbance." It was just about four o'clock when the governor came to our premises with a squad of soldiers, our message having elicited no response up to that time" (Barton, 1998 page 76). Again, the massacres began just after the noonday prayer of the Muslims to coincide with the affluent Armenians being in their open shops in the market, an incentive to local Muslims to participate in the massacres.

68   Kaloosdian describes an incident where Ashreff met on the road his teenage father, on the way to ask for refuge in the home of a friendly Turk, and Ashreff turned the boy back (2015, page 92).

69   Khayo Haroian was an in-law as well as a patriarchal clan head in Tadem. His daughter Mariam would survive through forced marriage to a Turk (Bedros Haroian, 2021, page 178). His daughter-in-law Bado would also enter into a forced marriage to survive (Bedros Haroian, 2021, pages 112, 178, 181, 182, 183). His son Haykaz, educated in Mezre to be a teacher, was one of the first victims of the Genocide along with his father (Bedros Haroian, 2021, pages 27, 38, 39, 112, 133).

70   Crushing of heads was another common form of torture, with the Turks even inventing a special kind of vice for the purpose: "They put their hands and heads in a sort of pinching machine until the bones crack and break" (Jacobsen, 2001, page 65). However, in villages or other remote locations, the head crushing vices were not always available. One Protestant missionary describes the murder of a leading Protestant in the Armenian community: [He] "...was killed openly by having his head crushed by heavy stones beaten against it" (Harris, 1897, page 241).

71   Kaloosdian gives the specific location in Tadem for collections: Chatal Fountain (2015, page 89) and date (early July) (2015, page 94) and estimates of the collection of women and children that time to be three hundred (2015, page 95). Of those 300 deported, "perhaps twenty-five were ever delivered to the Deir el-Zor" (2015, page 114).

72   The Toomasians were one of the four "yerli" (founding) families along with the Haroians, Bogoians, and Elloians (Kaloosdian, 2015, page

14). Their land holdings and social status would have been significant before the genocidal campaigns were launched, a process that included not only the 1894-1896 Great Massacres and the 1915 Genocide but the regular individual injustices against Armenians who showed leadership or bravery or who had significant wealth or desirable females. Kaloosdian observes, "My father, Boghos, recalled that every time they used the road that bordered their farms, someone would lament, "This land was ours. This orchard was ours" (2015, page 31).

73 Ashreff as noted was the son of Ibosh and grandson of Hadji Bego, who lead the Great Massacres (Kaloosdian, 2015, page 18). His uncle Hafiz would lead the Genocide, and so Ashreff's threats would have thrown Guleeg Haroian into emotional upheaval. That Guleeg had brought food ("chicken and what-not") for the deportation indicates her initial decision was to risk the deportation, but the threat of the murderer, torturer, and rapist Ashreff changed her decision: "I jumped.... I ran.... I escaped." A threat from Ashreff portended not only death but also a cruel death, and Guleeg Haroian must have been terrified.

74 "Hagop's sister" is likely Margaret Vanetzian, née Haroian. Hagop Haroian had three sisters: an older sister who married into the Narzhonts clan (modernized name, Najarian). The Narzhonts/Najarian clan had Kurdish kin, and the standard course of action during the Genocide would have been to shelter with the Kurdish kin. Kaloosdian mentions a Najarian family who did go to a Kurdish village (2015, page 293). A second sister married a Nordigian, who seems to have been long departed Tadem by the time of the 1915 Genocide. The third sister, Margaret, married a Vanetzian and remained in Tadem. In Bedros Haroian's *Memoirs of a Soldier about the Days of Tragedy*, only Margaret figures prominently.

75 The officials' threat was a literal statement of government policy. The prosperity of the 'infidel' Armenians goaded the Turks, making highly popular the government decision to steal Armenian wealth to finance

the war effort and to build a new Muslim middle class. For a summary, see Footnote 31, "Economic Motives: The Great Massacres and Genocide" (Haroian, Bedros, 2021, page 372).

76   The Young Turk government shielded local *aghas* such as Hafiz who sold Armenian women and children. For example, Turkish scholar Taner Akçam notes that a government official had to clear up confusion over an order that Muslims who had been hiding Armenians be executed and their houses burned: that "penalty does not apply to 'those who shelter or protect women and children…who have been officially distributed by the government to Muslim houses'" (2018, page 17).

77   "Bread" refers to Armenian 'cracker bread.' Cracker bread is a thin and crispy round bread (about 18 inches in circumference). This dry Armenian bread keeps for several weeks. To eat, a person sprinkles the bread with water to soften it up. Most Mediterranean (and other cultures with dry summers and cold winters) have a similar dried bread that is sprinkled or quickly dipped in water before serving, for example Italian *friselle* bread.

78   Villages used a town crier, a *mounedig*.

79   Scholarship confirms that attackers carried off women considered attractive but robbed and killed any women deemed 'plain' (see for example Walker, 1980, pages 219, 223). In other words, women were like cattle or sheep at a village fair.

80   My grandmother—like other Armenians, male and female—does use the word "rape" when describing other females who are neither identified nor identifiable.

81   Village houses were "low and contiguous" (Greene and Northrop, 1896, page 157).

82   The Armenian "oven" was a *tonir*, a round hole in the ground, 4 - 5 feet deep, lined with stone. A main dish like *kavoormah* would cook

over the coals at the bottom while cracker bread dough was slapped on the sides and baked.

83 Ahmed was another of Hadji Bego's four sons. Like other Ottoman officials, his family would have been sure to claim the "biggest wealth" from the emptied Armenian houses.

84 Of the first six named, three more belonged to the *Hadji* Bego family: Hussein, Moheiddin, and Alosman. Moheiddin was one of Hadji Bego's four sons (Hafiz, Ahmed, Ibosh, and Moheiddin).

85 Multiple reports document the Turkish habit of stealing clothes and shoes during the Genocide. For instance, U.S. Consul Leslie A. Davis travelled the countryside on horseback to document the scenes of mass graves of ten thousand bodies or more and to provide details on the corpses: "A remarkable thing about the bodies that we saw was that nearly all of them were naked. I have been informed that the people were forced to take off their clothes before they were killed, as the Mohammedans consider the clothes taken from a dead body to be defiled. There were gaping bayonet wounds on most of the bodies, usually in the abdomen or chest, sometimes in the throat. Few persons had been shot, as bullets were too precious. It was cheaper to kill with bayonets and knives" (1989, 82-83). The last details suggest another reason to strip victims before killing them with bayonets and knives was to avoid damaging the clothing with holes and blood stains. The murderers further made it easy on themselves because stripping clothing off stiff dead bodies can be hard work. Finally, the murderers took a goof profit from selling the clothes of their murder victims (Davis, 2016, page 151).

86 Danish missionary Jacobsen details an encounter with "one of the leading Turks of Tadem, who stated that he had "enjoyed the Armenians' misery for a time. He had not taken anything from them as long as they were there, but when they had gone he had enjoyed their gardens

and vineyards," but he added that "sorrow" had since followed him (2001, page 140).

87   Kévorkian writes, "a kind of race then began between the authorities and the Turkish population to see who could plunder faster – doors, windows, and everything else were carried off" (2011, page 392; *see also* page 563 for locals recruiting school children to help in the race to steal Armenian goods, including windows, and page 607 for Armenian neighborhoods being transformed into "huge bazaars"). Prized were glass windows, given the poverty of many local Muslims and the comparative wealth of Armenians who had relatives in America. When Tademtzis in America raised funds to build a new school after the 1896 Great Massacres, it was considered the best in the province: "The new school had glass windows and 'because the building of the school was on high ground the classrooms were airy and bright'" (Kaloosdian, 2015, page 41). The Danish missionary in Mezre writes, "When the Armenians were sent away, the Turks plundered the houses, removing everything, including the doors and windows. Now these refugees must live in these open rooms. We cannot get windows. Glass can no longer be found, and we have no money to have frames made for paper to be stuck over them. The only hope we have for them is that the winter will be mild, so that they will not freeze to death" (2001, page 108). An American missionary in Kharpert notes that "doors and windows" were swiftly stolen from Armenian homes (Barton, 1998, page 69). The U.S. Consul, Leslie Davis, in Kharpert sums it up well: "The scene reminded me of vultures swooping down on their prey. It was a veritable Turkish holiday and all the Turks went out in their gala attire to feast and to make merry over the misfortunes of others" (1989, page 54).

88   Armenian women were not permitted to take their Armenian children into the household of their new Muslim husband but could transfer them to government orphanages for Turkification (*see also* "Editor's Introduction").

89   Memoirs are rife with accounts of the thieves pillaging homes while the occupants were still here. One example to illustrate only would be Shipley (1983, pages 62-63): "In this midst of this 'auctioning,' a huge officer appeared before mother. He told her that the mayor had sent his compliments and would like to take care of our organ during our exile. Because every time he passed our house and heard its soft music, he coveted it. Without any ado, with the help of two other brawny men, they picked up our organ and disappeared." An American missionary in Kharpert recounts, "I know that the mayor of the city frequently went on these searching expeditions and when he saw anything that he wanted, such as a bedstead or a rug, he peremptorily demanded it and the owner gave it simply because she dared not refuse it" (Barton, 1989, page 66).

90   Guleeg Haroian's use of "freedom" in the early 1900s in a remote Armenian village in the Ottoman Empire is not the same use as it would be in 21st century America. Kaloosdian writes on the Armenian response to the 1908 Young Turk revolution: "*Hurriyet* was Turkish for "liberty." But it was a kind of freedom they simply could not understand. They had long wished to be free of the tyranny of the Turks, but a true promise of equality was difficult to accept. They had not expected even a guarantee of safety, much less equality" (2015, page 45).

91   Witnesses to the prolonged torture of the Armenians during the 1915 Genocide sometimes exclaim that a three-day massacre would have been kinder. Riggs notes inflicting the prolonged suffering of the deportation was deliberate: "One of their leaders, the member of Parliament of whom I have already spoken, Hadji Mehmet Effendi of Harpoot, angered by a protest that I had made, spoke more frankly than he otherwise would have done when, before the beginning of the deportation from Harpoot, he said to me, 'The Armenians know what massacre is, and think they can bear that. But let them wait and see what deportation is. They never dreamed of being deported. They

will soon learn how much worse it is than massacre!' (1997, page 140). Danish missionary Jacobsen writes, "Time after time we hear people say, 'This time 20 years ago we had a massacre. It seemed to be terrible, but it was nothing compared to this. Then they ravaged for three days, and it was over, but this time it has gone on for months, and we cannot see an end to it'" (2001, page 70). She elaborates later on the deportation in the fall, "It would be much more merciful if they killed them at once, instead of taking them on journeys of several days in this cold and rain, without food or clothes…. The Turkish objective is simply to exterminate the Armenian nation with as much suffering as possible" (2001, page 113). An American missionary confesses to this thinking on a cold and rainy November night: "…I thought of all those women and children out on the mountains somewhere without shelter or food. Then the thought came, "Oh, I hope they have killed them before this!" Then, I was shocked at the thought, but why should I be? It is the only relief. Friends, homes, honor, and hope gone. Everything but life and a sure knowledge that it too must go sooner or later" (2000, page 61).

92 *Kavoormah* is a beef dish with two distinct variants. The fresh beef can be braised with onions and spices, or it can be 'dry fried,' meaning fried with oil to extract all the oils in the meat and produce a jerky-like beef that lasts longer. My grandmother would have made the latter, which, with the cracker bread, would have allowed her to stave off starvation of herself and her children for a few weeks at a minimum.

93 Leslie Davis, U.S. Consul in the region, comments in his report: "In addition to the bribery of officials the Turks who have kept Armenians in their houses have almost invariably demanded exorbitant sums for doing so. In very many instances they have kept them for a while and after getting all their money have turned them out to seek some other shelter" (published in Sarafian, 1995, page 139; see also Jacbosen, 2001, pages 93, 206, 213).

94   Guleeg Haroian employed a strategy to be absent from Tadem on the appointed days of deportation. For example, the Armenians everywhere were given notice "of the day when the occupants must leave. Two days are given for Mamouret-ul-Aziz, July 1st and third. Three days are given for Harput, July 4th, 5th, and 6th" (Davis, 1989, pages 52, 60; Sarafian, 1995, page 3; *see also* Morris and She'evi, 2019, page 193; Mouradian, 2021, page 136). After the first collection, when a notice was given to Tademtzi to go on a certain date, Guleeg Haroian would leave before that date and go to a neighboring village such as Yegheki (Personal Interview). Guleeg Haroian was outmaneuvering the Turks.

95   Derderian notes the purpose of stripping Armenians naked: "nakedness of female deportees contributed to their dehumanization in the eyes of the general population...." One group of naked Armenian women were herded at a train station temporarily, and "When the doors of the carriages were opened, they were jeered at by the populace for their nakedness" (2005, page 8). The whoremaster [use is literal] who put up for sale as sex slaves a group of 300 – 400 naked Armenian females in a market in Damascus repeatedly called out, "Rejoice oh ye faithful in the shame of the Christians" (*ibid*, page 12).

96   Note: My grandmother's words—"this kind of thing happened to us"—reminds one that rape was unspeakable.

97   Note: Again, "This and that happened" reminds one that the crimes inflicted on Armenian women were unspeakable.

98   "...escaped on the road" means that Yeva escaped from a Death March and fled back to the village to hide or self-rescue through forced transfer into a Muslim household (Yeva eventually manages the latter).

99   This sister is Takouhi.

100   Tachjian notes "...the Ottoman army had been the mainstay of survival for many Armenians, especially in the last phase of the war, when thousands of deported Armenian men and women had found

work in its workshops. In these structures they found themselves in semi-servitude; nevertheless, they received the daily nutrition that prolonged their survival (2019, pages 177-178; see also 2009, page 77).

101   The timing as well as Eva's description in her oral history indicates this was likely the "Saroutsna Sevkiat: The Massacre of the Remnants" described by Kaloosdian (2015, pages 123-131).

102   Eva reveals in her oral history that she informed the young official that her mother has married a Turk, i.e. converted to Islam.

103   Eva is showing herself to be clever, brave, and taking initiative, traits bundled into the word *jarbig* by Armenians. Miller and Miller note, "we frequently heard the expression *jarbig* in reference to children who survived" (1993, page 113). In her more recent study of child-survivor narratives, Maksudyan refines the definition of *jarbig* applied to child survivors: it translates into "agency," which "was mostly the capacity to endure and suffer" until that moment when the children could become "self-rescuers" (2018, page 22). Guleeg Haroian and her family defined *jarbig* as "she has no flies on her."

104   See footnote 23 for details on this ruse. The Vali, Sabit Bey, was keeping meticulous count of the number of deported Armenians. Out of the 51,000 Armenian who had been in his province, the Vali estimated 4,000 "were still hiding in the villages." Subsequently, "to find these fugitives and flush them out of their hiding places.... Vali Sabit needed to restore a climate of relative confidence." Vali Sabit Bey assured everyone that the last deportations were now over. In November, however, after the work of the harvest had been finished, the Turks flushed out and deported the remaining Armenians (Kévorkian, 2011, pages 400-401; Davis, 2016, pages 150 and 151-152 *see also* Kaloosdian, 2015, pages 123-131).

105   Harotiun Altounian was the father of Pilatzoon Altounian, who married Boghos Haroian (brother of Hagop Haroian). Harotiun

survived because he was in charge of transportation for the governor of the province.

106   The Armenian suffix "-tzi" means from, so a "Tademtzi" was someone from Tadem.

107   Eva describes her capture in her oral history: "Mother went out. The Turks came to gather again. They knocked on the door and yelled, 'You have to come out.' They came and pushed you away if you're hiding. We were in the fields, hiding under the big pile of straw. But they put their swords into that to find us. They hit one of us and gathered us. They took every single Armenian they could find away."

108   Herein Guleeg Haroian's efforts may have proved decisive, for it is far better to endure a forced march through desert in November than in July (Kaloosdian, 2015, page 94, Davis, 1989, page 52). In *Armenia: A Historical Atlas*, historian Robert Hewsen notes the 1915 deportations were timed in the summer, during the worst heat, with the destination for the handful of survivors being the Der-el-Zor desert concentration camp (page 233). The Turkish government timed with cruelty both the 1895 Great Massacres and the 1915 Genocide. Whereas the 1915 Death Marches (deportations) took place in the blistering heat of summer, the 1895 massacres had been timed in late October and early November, leaving the Armenian women, children, and old men in half-destroyed houses and with silos and stables robbed empty. Armenians who had survived the three days of killing of the Great Massacre would still die through cold and starvation or be forced to accept transfer into Turkish and Kurdish homes.

109   A report from the American Consul, Leslie Davis, in Kharpert, states well the observation made by many witnesses on the prolonged torment of the 1915 Genocide compared to the 1894-1896 Great Massacres: "A massacre, however horrible the word may sound, would be humane in comparison with it. In a massacre many escape but a wholesale deportation of this kind in this country means a lingering

and perhaps even more dreadful death for nearly every one" (published in Sarafian, 1995, page 3). The observations of U.S. Ambassador to Turkey, Henry Morgenthau, provide many examples of the impact of the "prolonged horror" of the deportees (2019, pages 319-310): "Such as escaped these attacks in the open would find new terrors awaiting them in the Moslem villages. Here the Turkish roughs would fall upon the women, leaving them sometimes dead from their experiences or sometimes ravingly insane" (1919, page 316).

110 Guleeg Haroian omits to mention her second Turkish husband, Moustafa Agha, who was sheltering her and Bado Haroian.

111 Doctor Mikahil was "a well established physician and surgeon" in Mezre (Atkinson, 2000, page ix). Western missionaries anglicized his name to Michael, e.g., the Danish missionary Jacobsen refers many times to "an Armenian doctor, Mr. Michael" in Mezre (Jacobsen, 2001, pages 9, 12, 57, 65, 75, 125-126, 246). That a prominent Armenian surgeon would be addressed by what Americans think of as a first name was not unusual in the Ottoman Empire, which did not have a surname law. The U.S. Consul, Leslie Davis, goes into detail to explain the fluidity in naming practices at that time, noting that Armenians in Kharpert "usually adopted as their surname the Christian name of their father" (1989, page 106). Later, when Guleeg Haroian travels to Mardin, she works with a "Dr. Garo" in the hospital, and "Garo" is an Armenian first name, short for Garabed (or Charles). Doctor Mikahil survived the Genocide and made it to America, where his son, J. Michael Hagopian, founded the Armenian Film Foundation and became an Emmy-nominated filmmaker for one of his many films documenting the Armenian Genocide.

112 Accounts of survivors who were separated from their children echo Guleeg Haroian's narrative of emotional collapse. Some parents had children caught separately from them. Some desperate parents sold a child to save her or him or to obtain bread to save their siblings.

Watenpaugh gives an example that serves as good illustration: "I saw a woman go mad a few hours after selling her two children. Others fell into a sort of lethargic, stupid state, their gaze distant, sitting for hours on the ground. You'd think that their feelings and consciousness were dead" (2013, page 285). Armenian females who had been rescued by Europeans from sexual outrage all showed "signs of severe trauma, like speechlessness or delirium, because of the abuse and because they had had to watch relatives getting their throats cut" (Bjornlund, 2009, pages 33 and 41).

113 Missionaries who witnessed the Genocide also write of emotional collapse (see *Okkenhaug*, 2010). Karen Jeppe, for example, was "sick and nerve racked," and she "never fully recovered her health; something had died inside her. Alma Johansson expressed the same sentiments. For her, even several years after the genocide the idea of continuing living was beyond endurance" (page 80). During the Genocide or at other times in Turkey, Bodil Biørn used scripture references to describe her emotional state. For example, in a letter home, Biørn referred to "Ps 69, 2-4" which states, "I sink in deep mire, where there is no standing: I am come into deep waters, where the floods overflow me. / I am weary of my crying: my throat is dried; my eyes fail while I wait for my God" (page 82).

114 Survivors note when Turks or Kurds who perpetrated the Genocide or the Great Massacres ask casually for bread. For example, Bedros Haroian recounts an incident in his *Memoirs of a Soldier About the Days of Tragedy*: "One day when Manoog *amu's* wife Hrop was baking bread, *Hadji* Bego, who was walking by, smelled the nice aroma and walked in, saying, "Good morning, Hrop *khanum*. You know, I am hungry. Could you give me some bread to eat?" Hrop gave him two pieces of bread and said, "Here you go, *agha*. Take the bread." But she thought to herself, "The hell with you, beast. You killed my brother-in-law Hovhanes, and now you have come and are asking for bread. Let you die. Let you be like your son who died howling"

(2021, page 28). Others note this kind of casual cruelty. For example, the Turks who had slaughtered the Armenians smiled "triumphantly" whenever they passed a survivor in the streets (Harris, 1897, page 70). An American missionary in Kharpert notes that the wife of the governor *(vali)* Sabit Bey, who was responsible for the death of tens of thousands of Armenians, proposed that the American missionary promise her little girl to be "the wife of her little son when they are grown" (Atkinson, 2000, page 56).

115   "*Kharpertzi*" meant someone from Kharpert (also pronounced Harpoot), the *vilayet* (province) in which Tadem was located.

116   In *Memoirs of a Soldier*, Bedros Haroian identifies Guleeg and Bado's exact location. Bedros Haroian has escaped, and Moheiddin, the brother of Hafiz and son of Hadji Bego, is hunting him down: "As I later discovered, Moheiddin and Huseyn did go to the authorities and reported that a revolutionary Bedros had arrived to Mezre the night before and was staying at Tevrish Mahla Khochapach's house. They felt certain of my location because my two sisters-in-law had lived in Moustafa's house for months."

117   U.S. Consul, Leslie Davis, author of *The Slaughterhouse Province: An American Diplomat's Report on the Armenian Genocide, 1915-1917*. Ed. Susan K. Blair. New Rochelle, NY: Aristide D. Caratzas, Publisher, 1989.

118   Garabed Bedrosian, translator and bodyguard to U.S. Consul Leslie A. Davis (Atkinson, 2000, pages ix-x).

119   Skilled Armenian tradesmen—bakers, waggoneers, millers, and so on—could be exempted from the deportations, and they constituted their own network of aid for the small numbers of Armenians who had evaded the collections.

120   Illiteracy—not literacy—was the norm in the Ottoman Empire.

121   Scholarship that investigates the "lived experiences" of female Armenian survivors through their "microhistories" (Bilal, 2019,

185) describes the conditions that left "no life" for them. For women who were transferred into Muslim homes before they had children or, tragically, lost all their children, conditions that made their lives unbearable were constantly hiding their Armenian identities to protect against "verbal attacks from neighbors" and being unable to discuss the Genocide from fear of the consequences of doing so (Bilal, 2019, pages 188, 198, 199). After the war, official harassment of Armenians continued as the Committee of Union Progress ("Young Turks") simply reorganized "under new names, such as *Hurryet Itilaf* (Liberal Entente) and "Association of Kurdistan" (2011, page 748).

122   Again, illiteracy was the norm in the Ottoman Empire, so testimonies were still largely oral.

123   Dikranogerd was the Armenian name for the city the Turks refer to as Diyarbekir. "Dikranogerd" means "Built by [King] Dikran."

124   Guleeg is referring to a city that now bears the Turkish name Diyabakir.

125   *Bey* is another Ottoman title.

126   This was a common tactic. Many Armenians made others their primary relatives to give and to receive help. See for example Kaloosdian, 2015, page 113: When an Armenian named Seghpos hears of some surviving Tademtzi women working in a village, he sent a letter to the village *mukhtar's* son asking that his "sisters" be sent to him in Mosul.

127   Guleeg Haroian is describing some kind of blood pudding, cake, or sausage.

128   For a summary on the slave markets for Armenian women and children, see "Sale of Women and Children" (footnote 152) in Bedros Haroian's *Memoirs of a Soldier about the Days of Tragedy* (pages 410-411). *See also* Balakian, Peter, 2003, page 192. Trafficking in "slave-markets" was also prevalent during the 1894-1896 Great Massacres as was distributing women and girls to the soldiers (Lepsius, 1897, pages 28-29; Keiser, 2018, pages 185, 240, 290).

129 Guleeg Haroian is also exhibiting the trait of being *jarbig* (see footnote on page 201 for definition within context of 1915 Armenian Genocide).

130 *Cross-reference:* In "Bones and Bodies, We Had To Walk Over Them…" Eva describes the use of clothing as a survival strategy by her Aunt: "Aunt Marnos had worn two dresses, one of top of the other. The nice clothes underneath were all pleated and white. Aunt Marnos had on pants called *shalvars*. The nice clothes were in the *shalvars*. Every night when we went by a village, she tore a part of her nice dress. She cut one nice piece of white cloth—material for ladies—and we went and exchanged it for food with ladies. We did not have any money. The women had food, but they wanted us to give them something before they gave us any food."

131 Again, "my house" is a reference to the clan system.

132 Saint Gregory the Illuminator (a Parthian noble) succeeded in converting the nation of Armenia to Christianity in 301 A.D. Other Armenian churches–such as Catholic or Protestant–are smaller and founded later, primarily from missionary work in the Ottoman Empire in the 1880s. The numbers of Catholics and Protestants began to grow from operating soup kitchens after the Great Massacres of 1894-1896.

133 The participation of Armenian women in the *vorpahavak* ("collection of orphans") was critical because those who had taken the Armenian children during the Genocide told them, "…the Americans had come to steal them, and this represented a new disaster. They remembered the terror of separation from their others four years earlier" (Mouradian, 2021, page 84). Moreover, though the British supported reclamation of Armenian brides and children, "Armenian authorities themselves had to organize to carry out the rescue missions" (Kévorkian, 2011, page 760).

134 Toros' decision to run away would have been 'wise' for a child. Many Armenians who survived did so by escaping the collections, repeatedly. Darbinyan quotes Dr. Semin, Russia, who spoke of "'savage-like

children,' who would avoid any contact with humans and run away like "'beasts'" (2020, page 15). His wife and nurse noted the children's "big black eyes were enormously brisk, filled with animal fear, seeking a shelter to escape to and hide" (Darbinyan, 2020, page 15). For a summary analysis of the Turkish methods of slaughtering the Armenian children, see Dadrian (2003): the child survivors were collected and killed by three primary methods: drowning operations, burning alive, and wholesale rapes of the girls and the boys, after which they were systemically murdered. The burning alive and other tortures of children could take place in front of large crowds and Turkish notables to impress them with the urgent need to erase the Armenians from the Ottoman Empire. *See also* Mouradian, 2021, pages 136-138.

135   This may have been the Melkon mentioned earlier, son of Yeva (Guleeg's niece).

136   Guleeg Haroian's oldest living grandchild, Thomas Tashjian, noted that she had told him the government "heard the case and decided that Eva had to go with Grandma." When the Ottoman Empire lost the war, the Young Turk leaders fled the country on 1 November 1918. The new government curried favor for better terms of the Armistice through acts such as ordering all captive Armenian females and children returned to their families (*see for example* Ekmekcioglu, 2013, page 533). Ekmekcioglu notes the Armenian survivors engaged in the *vorpahavak*, the gathering of orphans, "did not shy away from using force, frequently under the protection of British or French soldiers" (Ekmekcioglu, 2016, page 38). Eva's adoptive father was a prominent citizen in Mardin, but he may have been reluctant to go publicly against the Allied forces occupying the city.

137   Both sides of the conflict were fighting hard to draw Post-WWI boundaries in the region. The last British train left Aleppo during the 1919 transfer of some territories to the French (who would soon abandon the attempt to govern Mardin). Adana—the destination of the train car

with the Turkish husbands—would end up on the Turkish side of the border. Aleppo—the destination of the train car with the Armenian brides—would end up on the Syrian side of the border.

138   My grandmother's description of the *vorpahavak*, collecting the orphans, is typical of the accounts given by others (*see* for example Miller and Miller, 1983, pages 122-123).

139   Eva elaborated that later on the young women were sent to marry Armenian husbands in Adana (capital city of Cilicia) (Hightaian, Personal Interview). The British and French had re-patriated about tens of thousands of Armenian refugees from the desert concentration camps to Cilicia, and the French brought in Armenian Legionnaires to control the region's banditry, etc. During these months in Cilicia, many Armenian men would have begun to establish themselves in Cilicia. Moreover, survivors flocked to Allied-occupied territories such as Adana and Constantinople that were safer for them (Ekmekcioglu, 2016, page 23).

140   The Passenger List for Ellis Island includes Guleeg and Eva (spelled slightly incorrectly) arriving on February 12 on the Rochambeau which sailed from Le Havre, France on January 31, 1920.

141   Guleeg Haroian is showing clear skill in oral delivery. Her oral history is episodic, not unlike *The Odyssey* or Chaucer's *Canterbury Tales*, with community story telling clues inserted (e.g., "We went long, we went little."). The oral culture of the villages was quite different from 21st century writing cultures. For example, the villagers were frequently multilingual though they could not read or write, and they were experienced in capturing history orally (for instance, Homer delivering *The Odyssey*). The oral culture of the villages is likely a contributing factor to the lack of accounts from females in the villages and even in some towns and cities. Even Eva's adoptive mother, an Arab from a high-class family, could not read or write.

142   Tachjian covers name changes en masse when entire Armenian communities were forced to convert (2019, see for example pages 162 - 165).

143   This mentality persists in Turkey today. Ekmekcioglu writes, "It should be noted that among Turkish Muslim citizens in Turkey, having Armenian ancestry is still widely considered shameful, and the person potentially disloyal. *"Ermeni dölü"* (Armenian sperm) is still used as an insult (2013, page 552). Ekmekcioglu proceeds to give examples, including the demonization of Hrant Dink that led to his assassination in 2007.

144   Gang rapes were so vicious that the females died: "...outraged with such accompaniments of nameless brutality that their agonies often culminate in a horrible death. Girls of eleven and twelve—nay, of nine—are torn from their families and outraged in this way by a band of 'men' whose names are known, and whose deeds are approved by the representatives of law and order" (see for example Pierce, 1896, pages 411, 423). Morris and She'evi similarly note the rapes of women and girls, aged 12 – 40 (2021, page 82).

145   *Rayah* translates loosely as cattle and refers to infidels/non-Muslims (those Syrians who were Christians).

146   Despite Eva's equivocal response to her mother, Guleeg Haroian does offer complete and unconditional support for Eva to leave. That may have been as critical as having a relative in America. Miller and Miller studied the oral histories of surviving women, and one of the conclusions drawn is applicable: "By the end of the deportation journey, all her support structures had completely disappeared...." Eva suddenly had her mother supporting her to leave.

147   A reminder here is that Armenians used the word "Turke" to describe Muslims in the Ottoman Empire. The "village Turks" thus includes the Kurdish aghas appointed by the Ottoman authorities.

148 Peroomian notes, "Almost all of the survivors spoke of nightmares haunting them and affecting their behavior. The horrors they experienced live on in the deep layers of their memory and are propelled to the surface in their sleep, when the willful suppression of these images is not functioning" (2009, page 13). MacKeen provides these final words on her Armenian grandfather: "Somehow, he'd escaped the desert, but he would never escape the past" (2016, page 278).

149 The 1908 Revolution allowed free travel. Before, the Armenians had strict local internal passports (*teskereh nufus*) and lived as hostages in the Ottoman Empire. If the Armenians sought to travel, they had to engage in significant bribery and secrecy. Some Armenians could obtain passports through "large bribes" while others travelled clandestinely (see for example Morris and She'evi, 2019, page 127). When the travel restrictions loosened, that also meant that those who had managed to make it to the U.S. before 1908 could more easily return to the Ottoman Empire (Kaloosdian, 2015, page 48).

150 This aside is included to illustrate the silence under which survivors buried their emotional nightmare. Local killers will murder savagely the grandmother of Eva—and Rose—during the Genocide. Rose was born in America, and found crushing silence instead of family stories.

151 Khardalian similarly encounters resistance to discussing the names (*Grandma's Tattoos*, 21:00 – 22:50).

152 Eva's analogy to *Rawhide* is fitting as the region was akin to the lawless Wild West in the 1700s and 1800s in the U.S. *Rawhide* was an American Western television series portraying the challenges of trail bosses and drovers of cattle drives (hence the name of the show, *Rawhide*).

153 Before the 1908 Revolution, a legal prohibition prevented the Armenians and other non-Muslims from bearing arms. One result was that the Armenians defended themselves by wielding clubs and similar instruments as well as improvised instruments (Haroian, 2021, footnote 48, page 379).

154   One missionary describes life in Armenian villages: "No drones were tolerated in that busy hive, and in all their toil men and women stood shoulder to shoulder" (Greene and Northrop, 1896, page 162).

155   The adults of course had stunningly clear memories of the 1894-1896 Great Massacres: "Five hundred thousand Armenians put to death or dying of starvation! This moment, while I speak, all up and down Armenia sit many people, freezing in the ashes of their destroyed homes, bereft of most of their households, and awaiting the club of assassination to put them out of their misery" (Pierce, 1896, page 339). Francis E. Clark, D.D., President of the United Society of Christian Endeavor, bemoaned that one could only look upon the Great Massacres with "shuddering horror" (*ibid*, page 355). One missionary notes of the survivors of the Great Massacres, which occurred from 1894-1896: "And now Harpoot is trembling. The fiery trial of November last was not enough. The Turks are saying 'Wait a little, wait until the harvest is gathered in. By the middle of October this will be done, and then——.' Imagine with what feelings the peasants are reaping their fields, and the poor wives and daughters are doing about their daily tasks!" (1897, page 207).

156   U.S. Consul to Kharpert, Leslie Davis, during the genocide uses "konak" to describe a Turkish palace (page 60). Pierce goes into more detail. He notes, "A Turkish Konak is a large building, very irregular in construction and without the slightest approach to European ideas of comfort or convenience" and then describes the rooms, floors, building materials, and so on (1896, pages 148-149). This *konagh* was the mansion of the governmental overseer of Tadem, named Hadji Bego, who had become rich on two decades of killing, assaulting, and robbing the Armenians in Tadem. Bedros Haroian describes in his *Memoirs* that Hadji Bego not only murdered a rich Armenian and stole his fortune, but also he used forced labor of the Armenian villagers to build his new manor: "During the massacres, Bego called his looters, broke into Minas' house at night, and strangled him. Bego broke into

Minas' cellar and stole all his money. After, he destroyed Mano's house and built a new one, again forcing the backs of Armenian people" (2021, pages 14 and 20; *see also* Lepsius, 1897, pages 125-126).

157 Hovanes Der Hovanessian survived and was the father of Diana Der Hovanessian, a poet who won national and international awards, was on the translation board of Columbia University, and lectured on the literature of human rights. Hovanes was a high school student in Mezre when he was brought in and tortured (Kaloosdian, 2015, pages 76-77). He later escaped, and his daughter Diana later wrote a poem about the torture of her grandmother, Zarif, when she refused to reveal the hiding place of her son. The Turks smashed her right arm, flayed it, and then chopped it off (*About Time*, 1987, pages 24-25).

158 As noted, before 1908, Armenian men could not bear arms, but they were allowed to wear a sword on their wedding day to fight against the widespread stealing and raping of young Armenian brides by Turks and Kurds. These colors suggest this may be a wedding day sword (draped with red, green, and white ribbons). A crown made of red, green, and white threads was placed on the heads of the bride and groom, with green signifying life, red signifying sacrifice, and white signifying peace. Grooms also wore embroidered sashes of red and green pinned to white shirts. The embroidered images may enhance the symbolism, e.g., by using symbols such as grapes, pomegranates, and wheat to represent prosperity, wealth, and health.

159 Kaloosdian notes that Armenians were encouraged by the 1908 Revolution, but in 1909 came news of the massacres of Armenians in Adana: "The news of Adana caused some Tadem men to draw up protection plans should similar violence spread to their area" (2015, page 48). The conscription of Armenian men with the outbreak of World War I undermined these plans.

160 The image of a young woman (Guleeg Haroian) and her three children hiding a sword witnesses the insights of the German Pastor Johannes

Lepsius. When he reported on the Great Massacres, he wrote: "We ask again: 'Does a right of self-defence exist?' If so, will the Armenians be regarded as a reprobate band of brigands if they should contemplate a national rising? But, Heaven be thanked, say the diplomatists, we have just heard that the Armenians are in no condition to take such action, for fortunately they lack the two necessaries, food and arms. But how if some power who possesses both money and weapons should think of giving the Armenians what they want. *The third thing necessary, desperate courage, will not be wanting* [emphasis mine]. For whether they die with their last crust of bread in their hands, or armed for defensive fight, it will be a matter of indifference to them" (1897, pages 148-149). Lepsius' insight reveals what might be the most compelling reason that the nation of Armenia exists today. The vastly outnumbered Armenians, many half-starved survivors, fought with "desperate courage" to create their own country. *They were prepared to die, no matter the how.* The genius of the Dashnaktsutiun ("Dashnak") party that declared the First Republic of Armenia was understanding this. The Dashnaks inspired Armenian villagers with this promise: *They no longer had to die like slaves: They could die like heroes.* On an individual level, the words of an Armenian leader, H. Khorasanjian, sum it up: "If we must perish, let us be cut down with honor: let us assume our responsibilities and die behind our breastworks" (Kévorkian, 2011, page 155).

161 Herein we see the child's perspective of Eva. She is accurate but does not identify the 1908 Revolution that promised reforms and led her father and brothers to end to the practice of sexually abusing Armenian females.

162 Kévorkian quotes Turkish Grand Vizier, Halmi Pasha, on the Armenians desire for 'freedom' under the despotic "old regime": "… its sole aim was to achieve emancipation from the unbearable harassment and misdeeds of a despotic government" (2011, page 105). Eva's statement, "We had found our freedom" confirms this definition: after

the 1908 Revolution, the Armenians could stand up to abuses such as the chronic rape of their women.

163 "… this group or that group" refers to the political parties that Armenians were finally able to participate in openly after the 1908 Revolution.

164 Kaloosdian describes the Ottoman government requisitioning animals and forcing the remaining old men or boys to transport goods: "Kevork and the Oxcarts: Requisition and Exhaustion" (2015, pages 61-68).

165 "In the Deserts of DerZor" ["DerZor Collerinde"]. In 2017, a PBS station recorded a modern performance to commemorate the 10th anniversary of the assassination in Turkey of Hrant Dink, an Armenian journalist and human rights advocate: https://www.pbs.org/video/armenian-lamentation-song-derzor-collerinde-14427/.

166 Again, Armenian females were plunder for Muslim males. If they entered into a marriage with a Muslim, the Armenian female had to eradicate her Armenian identity, which included surrendering her Armenian children to a Muslim orphanage where the officials would erase the children's Armenian identity and indoctrinate them to be Muslims.

167 Hagop Haroian had three sisters. The oldest was married to a Najarian, another was married to a Nordigian, and the third was married to a Vanetzian. The sister mentioned here was most likely Margaret Vanetzian (née Haroian). In *Memoirs of a Soldier about the Days of Tragedy*, Bedros Haroian mentions his sister Margaret consistently. Of the two older sisters, Narjarian had Kurdish relatives and would likely have taken refuge with them, and Nordigian seems to have been absent from Tadem, perhaps having immigrated years before to America.

168 This is the first of four critical moments in which Eva's notes she held someone's hand. Jinks identified the significance of holding someone's hand in critical moments (2022).

169 "Kulangants" is the clan name. Not until 1934 did a surname law come into effect in Turkey (Göçek, 2015, page 305). Naming conventions were not set in 1800s in the Ottoman Empire. Today's standard "-ian" for Armenian surnames was not the standard during the time of this memoir. "-ian" is used alternately with "onts," "enk," "ents," "ants," and similar endings designating clan names. For example, "Hagopian" might also appear as "Hagopents," and both deriving from the Christian name ("Hagop") of the clan headman.

170 The currency was gold, and females frequently wore some of their family's wealth according to status.

171 Bedros Haroian identifies Yousouph *agha* as Yeva's protector (2021, page 178). Yousouph is a common Muslim name, yet there were only 10 Turkish families in Tadem, so of note is that Kaloosdian identifies a Yousouph *agha* who had married an Armenian woman, who hid Armenians in 1915. So thorough was the indoctrination of Armenians captured in Muslim households that when Kaloosdian interviewed Ayoub (Yousouph's son) decades later, Ayoub had no idea his mother was Armenian (2015, pages 280-281).

172 This is the Yeva, Guleeg's niece, who escaped a collection and managed to walk back to the village, carrying her young son Melkon on her shoulders. The fate of Yeva and her child is illustrative. Yeva finally entered the household of Yousouph *agha* for protection (Haroian, Bedros, 2021, page 178). At some point, Yeva and her small son may have been separated. Children playing, running errands, or at work were routinely swept up in collections. Further on in this oral history, Guleeg Haroian names the children in rags and covered in sores that she picked up from the streets and alleys of the city of Mardin and carried to the Red Cross, and among those children is "Melkon" from the village. Similarly, the "sister" Bado with whom Guleeg Haroian was sheltering in the Turk Moustafa *agha*'s house also became separated from her son, Arakel (Bedros Haroian, 2021, page 182). The ending

for Yeva and her son Melkon and for Bado and her son Arakel was highly atypical: both mothers and sons were reunited in America. Arakel survived the Death March when a Kurd snatched him away to be a worker, and Arakel later escaped and went to the U.S. in 1923, separately but in the same time frame as his mother Bado, who succeeded in reaching the U.S. in 1923 when Turkey finally let Armenians leave (Kaloosdian, 2015, pages 290-291). More often, the fate of the separated children was terrible, with the children dying alone, abandoned, abused. One Armenian woman, Badaskhan Kezerian, who had transferred into a Muslim household to save her very young son Nishan, saw the unwanted boy raped and murdered by having his head slammed into the hard ground (Kaloosdian, 2015, page 163).

173 Graveyards were common collection points. The Danish Missionary in Mezre notes all the sick Armenians were rounded up in an old Turkish burial ground because it was surrounded by high walls and they could not escape: they could only die a slow, agonizing, and horrendous death (Jacobsen, 2001, pages 86-87). Another American missionary in Kharpert writes in despair, "Later, the exile camps were put in a cemetery—a very appropriate place. They had not far to be carried" (Barton, 1998, page 68).

174 "Turke" is Armenian word used to denote Ottoman Muslims, be they Turk, Kurd, Arab, Chechen, and so on. Bedros Haroian in *Memoirs of a Soldier about the Days of Tragedy*, identifies this woman as Khanum Kilivchan, the second wife of Hadji Bego. Unlike her husband, Kilivchan was a kind woman who with her brother was running a micro-underground railroad to help Armenians escape from Tadem to his Kurdish village of Kamishlu (2021, page 177).

175 Some Armenians were held in the villages "to do the work of harvest time" and these Armenians clung to the hope of survival, but they would find themselves collected and deported post-harvest (Riggs, 1997, page 173).

176   Guleeg Haroian does not possess the knowledge that when the war broke out, funds sent by Armenians in America were embargoed by the Turks, "never to be returned" (Kaloosdian, 2015, page 35).

177   The timing and description indicate this was likely the "Saroutsna Sevkiat: The Massacre of the Remnants" described by Kaloosdian (2015, pages 123-131). The government authorized Ouzoun ("Tall") Hassan to "capture the remaining Armenians and lead them to the killing site [Saroutsin] where they could be disposed of" (page 123). The Armenians were flushed out, rounded up, and followed by "a large and unruly angry mob from Turkish villages" (including Tadem). A survivor described the scene: "This was a slaughterhouse—brutality at its worst. Hassan and the other killers were local gendarmes, not professional soldiers or executioners, and that made them all the more savage. There were no piercing sounds of rifles or pistols. Instead, swords sliced and slashed against throats, clubs bludgeoned heads, stones were hurled at the dead and dying, knives stabbed defenseless persons—on and on as the bodies fell" (page 126).

178   Again, we see the value of my grandmother's strength and experience as head of household for so many years. She has skill with caretaking and butchering farm animals, including large ones such as cows, and this gave her the knowledge and experience to bandage the wounded. Kaloosdian notes that a handful of the survivors managed to return to Tadem, a few with hideous wounds such as sliced necks (2015, pages 129-130).

179   The Young Turk government sometimes spared Armenian tradesmen such as wagoneers, bakers, or butchers due to high demand for their skills. Not infrequently, those who endured, such as a butcher Guleeg Haroian later mentions, had converted to Islam.

180   The Vali, Sabit Bey, was Sabit Cemal Sağirzade (alternately Sağiroğlu with the Turkish suffix "oğlu" for "son of" Sağir). Vali Sabit Bey became notorious for his duplicity with the Armenians in his governance,

wholesale thieving of Armenian property, and the murder of hundreds of thousands of deportees passing through his province. *See* page 40, footnote 61.

181 Auburn and Leicester are suburbs of Worcester, Massachusetts, where Eva lived. Both suburbs are five to six miles away.

182 Survivor and witness testimonies abound with descriptions of abandoned children on the Death Marches. One survivor provides a graphic description: "…on a small rise, therefore roughly on a level with my eyes, a female child of about two years, only clothed with a red bodice which is pulled up. Bleeding genitals revealed and facing the street" (McKeen, 2016, page 141). Danish missionary Jacobsen writes, "Even young girls at the age of five are taken off the streets and misused terribly. Now is it so common that it happens in the open. What will be the end of it?" (2001, page 201). An American missionary in Konia writes, "I saw in the hospital one little girl, six years old, who had been brutally torn and mutilated by the fiendish lust of the Turkish soldier" (Barton, 1998, page 149). The Young Turk government did not want to waste costly bullets on a child, so death would have been manual: "Large numbers of children were smashed against walls and boulders" (Kévorkian, 2011, page 419; *see also* page 606). In general, round up sites for deportees became a "graveyard for … the small children abandoned by their mothers because they could no longer carry them" (Kévorkian, 2011, page 441-442). Surviving orphans were collected and "some of them were blown up in their carts with dynamite in an utterly uninhabited spot in the desert, while others were put in natural cavities in the ground, sprinkled with kerosene, and burned alive" (Kévorkian, 2011, page 667). Kerop Bedoukian, himself a deportee, provides a description of abandoned children: "I was fast on my feet, I could fly, wriggle, run, or crawl through any thickness of packed crowd, so I decided to go see what else was going on down below. I skipped, hopped, and threaded my way through the main crowd and entered a dense forest from where I could hear a new

sound, familiar in its distress but unfamiliar in its tone. This was a real forest: no bushes, flat ground, tall trees every ten feet or so. There was not a tree in my vision that did not have at least five children in its shade. What was strange was the absence of mothers; there were, however, a few women, crazed and not knowing what was going on. One woman was sitting under a tree in the midst of the children, moving from side to side, staring at the ground, expressionless. Two women appeared and went from tree to tree, picked up a child, and went back to the crowd. I myself felt weird. Under one tree there were six children from newly born to five or six years old. Three of the children were, or seemed to be, dead, as their neither cried nor moved. A fourth was whimpering, exhausted from hunger, thirst, and crying. The other two were letting the world know that they needed help. It was their combined, hopeless cry that I had heard from the distance. Under another tree a boy about five has plastered himself with his own excretion, and the boy next to him, who was younger, was copying him" (1978, pages 27-28). Sometimes the children were collected for medical experiments or military games. One survivor describes "the game of swords," a contest wherein Turkish soldiers would plant their swords in the ground, blade up, and then grab one of the girls, gallop on their horses, and toss the girl onto a sword (Balakian, Peter, 2003, page 262). Derderian notes that bands of orphans, eight to twelve years old, survived through incredible fortitude (2020). Tragically, Elizabeth Haroian, barely four years old, was too young to survive on her own or in one of these bands.

183   Tadem was in the province of Kharpert, one of the six Eastern provinces that had a large Armenian population and were north of Arabia.

184   Again, an illustration that the word 'rape' was absent from everyday vocabulary.

185   When Eva refers to "Syria," she is indicating cities like Mardin that were full of Syrians at that time.

186 "Çete" was the Armenian word for the extralegal Special Organization units formed to exterminate the Armenians. The U.S. Consul gave the phonetic spelling and definition: "A "cheteh" is a convict who has been released from prison and furnished a gun" (1989, page 58). Extensive documentation exists of these "army of murderers" (Akçam, 2006, pages 134-136). The *Teşkilât-i-Mahusa*, Enver Pasha's Secret Security force, organized the "Special Organization" units. Enver Pasha worked with the primary architect of the Armenian Genocide, Talaat Pasha, Minister of Interior, and directed Enver Pasha's Secret Security forces to mobilize Kurds, Bedouin tribesmen, and vengeful Muslim refugees from the Balkan Wars, and to empty the prisons—especially and including murderers and rapists—to form the Special Organization's "irregular units." Their work was to massacre the Armenians out of sight. The "çetes" needed little to no incentive to rob and kill, but they were provided an incentive: They were assured that they were participating in a *jihad*, a holy war, carrying out a "sacred religious obligation" to kill the infidels (Rogan, 2018, pages 160, 164, 173, 388; Balakian, 2009, page 95, 100). The Special Organization gangs "perpetrated the greatest crimes" (Akçam, 2006, pages 134-136). The deported Armenians named them well: Death Squads.

187 The cruelest murderers also bayoneted pregnant women in the 1894-1896 Great Massacres as well (Pierce, 1896, page 336). Similarly, sport was made of murdering fetuses and babies: "To play ball with a baby, and toss it from one bayonet to another before its mother's eyes seemed pleasant sport for the soldiers of Bitlis" (Lepsius, 1897, page 24-25). One Kurd confirmed that he had seen Turkish soldiers "'joking around' a pregnant woman and making 'bets as to the sex of her child. She was then cut open and the money was paid to the scoundrel who had guessed rightly" (Morris and She'evi, 2019, page 64). Another witness noted, "they cut open mothers with child, and tossed little children from knife to knife" (2021, page 96). The practice is not unique throughout the human history. Derderian observes on

1915 that "pregnant women, infants, and small children were often targets of violence as the embodiment of biological continuity," and a number of informants "saw or heard of pregnant women whose bellies were slit open or stabbed" (2005, page 9; *see also* Bjornlund, 2009, page 26). American missionaries recount similar instances (*see for example* Barton, 1998, page 178). Targeted were mothers of boys, the latter representing future Armenian resistance. Women who had undergone forced intermarriage and conversion were not allowed to take their Armenian children into the marriage but had to enter their Armenian children into a Muslim orphanage except for mothers of boys, who could be summarily deported no matter what the circumstance (Morgenthau, 1919, page 313; Derderian, 2005, page 10). Shipley in her memoirs provides details on both the targeting of mothers and of boys: "No guns were used unless someone tried to run. The victims were told they needed the bullets for the front. Swords, daggers, and rocks were used on most women. Pregnant women were slashed open to watch as their fetuses were pulled out and sliced into pieces, then left to bleed to death. Those who resisted were turned upside down, had their legs tied to two different branches, and then were split in half with an axe; their fetuses were chopped into bits. Crawling babies, whose mothers' heads had been smashed in, were thrown on the bodies of their mothers to suckle at their lifeless breasts. Small boys were tied together in fours and their heads crushed under heavy rocks" (1983, pages 67-68). *See also* Miller and Miller, 1993, pages 85 and 102.

188   Marnos' decision to leave her infant girl in a public location was not atypical during the Death Marches: "Two survivors told us independently that in front of a khan (inn) in Urfa, perhaps dozens of mothers placed their infants under a tree and walked on" (Miller and Miller, 1993, page 98). The decision to leave the babies in public places may have allowed these mothers to cling to the micro-thin hope that some local persons would adopt their babies. Other mothers clung to

their babies until they could "endure no more" and left them on the spot on "the mountains and roads to die a slow death. It is too painful to think about. No wonder that these mothers, if they survive such adversity, can never be comforted" (Jacobsen, 2001, page 149).

189   Yohaper was Eva's maternal cousin, the daughter of Guleeg Haroian's sister Khatun.

190   In Kharpert, the Armenians had been the "leaders and innovators in industry, especially the silk business" (Morris and She'evi, 201, page 190). Aunt Marnos was not the only Armenian who used clothing as a survival strategy. Kaloosdian's father survived by exchanging his fancy white *fisdan* for a small amount of money plus *khurma*, a pastry filled with dates that carried well on a journey (2015, page 196). Tachjian records the story of a woman, an accomplished tailor, who sold her embroideries to save her family (2019, pages 168-172). The desirability of Armenian clothing is ironic because the Sultan was the Caliph and the Ottoman Empire lived under Shari'a law, whose formal denigration of infidels included restricting the color of their clothing, the style of their shoes and headgear, and the quality of the fabrics to mark their inferiority (Akçam, 2006, page 24). The Armenians as a hard-working minority had survived through a strong work ethic and by developing portable skills. One result is that they were the prized tailors of the Ottoman Empire. Their ability to weave a quality muslin is evident here. *See also* Haroian, 2021, pages 34-36. Riggs notes that after the deportations, "... the price of cloth was terribly high. The Armenian merchants having been deported, the Turks were not able to carry on business very successfully, and so the supply of cotton cloth and of other cloth very soon gave out. The price of ordinary unbleached cotton cloth soon mounted to $2.50 a yard, and anything of any finer quality was even more expensive" (1995, page 156). Moreover, some Kurds attempted to stitch together the cloth stolen with "ludicrous" results (Riggs, 1997, page 178).

191   Survivor accounts note that adult Armenians often sent children on errands in the belief children would not be raped.

192   Eva Hightaian being on one the last Death Marches would have come across fields of corpses. Even though the Young Turks went to great lengths to hide their crimes, from using lime to burying the bodies in hastily dig ditches, most bodies were soon exposed. As one example to illustrate only, Balakian recounts in *Armenian Golgotha* his conversation with one Captain Shukri in charge of the Death Marches: "… Even though the Minister of Interior [i.e., Talaat] had huge ditches dug for the corpses, the winter floods washed the dirt away, and now the bones are everywhere, as you see" (2009, page 176). Accounts of both survivors and witnesses routinely mention similar incidents, e.g., having to cross "plains covered with Armenian corpses" (Rogan, 2015, page 178). Another survivor noted that as he climbed "over more corpses, the faces of death began to look the same. They were the remains of the hundreds of thousands preceding his convoy, Strange what the mind can become accustomed to" (MacKeen, 2016, page 108). He goes on that another deportee began counting the corpses, and "In one hour, the figure rose to five hundred, mostly girls, many partially consumed by wild dogs" (*ibid*, page 140; *see also* page 177). Examples abound to illustrate: "German officers and government functionaries travelling in the area in particular passed through the villages that had been used as 'fields of death'" (Akçam, 2018, page 160). "Meskene was filled with skeletons from one corner to the other; it simply took on the appearance of a field of bones" (*ibid*, page 210). A Venezuelan officer, Rafaël de Nogales, who had enlisted in the Ottoman Army, wrote he and a companion "had to jump our horses over the mountains of cadavers which obstructed our passage" (Kévorkian, 2011, page 338; *see also* pages 367, 505). Another survivor notes that some of the mounds of bodies were "unfortunately… as high as hills" (Kévorkian, 2011, pages 633, 656). Mouradian writes, "Mihran Zekiyan's convoy "walked over corpses from Ras ul-Ain to Meyadin for a week"" (2021,

page 132; *see also* page 185). One missionary wrote, "the corpses of Armenians are lying so thick on the main road that there are too many for the animals to eat" (2001, page 93; *see also* page 118), and she added on her colleagues: "The whole way they had travelled was a field of corpses, and there were places where they had to drive over them" (2001, page 116). Another writes, "Bodies lying on both sides of the road and sometimes the highway itself obstructed by the heaps of the dead. In one place for a space of about two rods, the road was covered with corpses over which Turks would force their horses to go rather than turn aside" (Barton, 1998, page 17). Yet another notes, "In the fall of 1915, after the widespread carnage, *hoja* Said, deputy from Harput, had traveled over the corpses of Armenians for three days on his way to Constantinople" (Balakian, Grigoris, 2009, page 120). The bodies strewn across the landscape were only a fraction because perpetrators dumped many bodies into the Euphrates River and one witness recounts the "thousands of dead bodies created such a barrage that the Euphrates changed its course for about a hundred yards" (Morgenthau, 1919, page 318). Finally, as nearly all men were killed immediately, many of the piles of corpses were children and women: "…along the entire trajectory of the railroad leading to Tell Abida and Ras ul-Ayn were piles of naked corpses of raped women" (2011, page 650).

193   This is a common theme in the literature of the Armenian Genocide. Of note is the Germans had already committed the first genocide of the 20th century on a smaller scale in 1904-1908 against the Herero and Nama tribes in Southwest Africa. The means were strikingly similar to the 1915 genocide of Armenians: collecting the tribes in makeshift concentration camps in the desert and preventing them from leaving so they died of dehydration, starvation, and disease (California State University, Fresno, "Genocides of the 20th Century," 1 September – 31 October 2018. See also https://library.fresnostate.edu/content/genocides-exhibition-2018).

194   Eva mentioned that her adoptive mother was descended from royalty and the family originally lived in the old castle on top of the hill in Mardin. Her adoptive father was also important, though "just an Effendi." When Guleeg Haroian learned of Eva's survival in Mardin and journeyed to reclaim her, the officials at the Refugee Tracing Center were hesitant to tell Guleeg Haroian where Eva was due to the power of her adoptive family and cautioned Guleeg that Eva may not accept her (Haroian, Personal Interview).

195   Diseases such as smallpox and German measles were still active at that time.

196   One day the jealous stepsister told Eva she was going to play a special game with her: she began to tattoo a bright blue dot on Eva's forehead. Eva's adoptive mother came in, stopped the tattooing immediately, and was very angry. That tattoo was the mark of a "low class Arab woman" (Hightaian, Personal Interview). Further research suggests it could also be the mark of sex slaves in the Arab culture, and Muslim women like Eva's stepsister attempting to tattoo her indicates the extent to which females were collaborators in the Genocide (Sanasarian, 1989, pages 453-454). At the time the underhanded stepsister tried to tattoo Eva, the Muslims were holding open sex slave markets of Armenian females, selling them for a pittance, in groups and individually, including in Mardin (Kévorkian, 2011, page 376). Should the stepsister have succeeded, and should Eva one day have become vulnerable again, Eva would have been branded for unspeakable practices. For a summary of scholarship on the slave markets for Armenian women and children, see "Sale of Women and Children" (footnote 152) in Bedros Haroian's *Memoirs of a Soldier About the Days of Tragedy* (pages 410-411).

197   Eva stipulating her name was "Shofkeeah" is a code: she had to undergo conversion to Islam, accept an Islamic name, and shed her Armenian identity (*see for example* Sarafian, 2010, pages 211-212; Ekmekcioglu, 2013, page 528-529). Later, Eva mentions that her adoptive father's

family had built the large mosque in the city of Mardin. Eva would have attended regularly—and publicly.

198   Miller and Miller studied the oral histories of surviving women, and one of the conclusions drawn is applicable to Eva [Hightaian] Haroian: "By the end of the deportation journey, all her support structures had completely disappeared.... She had struggled against insuperable odds to care for her children, and after their deaths she lost all sense of meaning in her life. She survived, however, because someone cared for her. These themes reverberate throughout our interviews, with substantial variations" (1993, page 97).

199   Mary as a girl was isolated and vulnerable. Gangs of Armenian male orphans monopolized locations and attacked anyone who dared approach their food source (e.g., dumpster) (Mouradian, 2021, 49), but Mary had only isolation and terror.

200   Eva spoke Armenian, Arabic, Turkish, and Kurdish, and (later) English. *Dhimmi* means non-Muslim, i.e., infidel.

201   Again, the moment of clasping hands seems significant in survivor histories (Jinks, 2022).

202   This "terrible famine" affected many child survivors (see for example Miller and Miller, 1993, page 116). One missionary writes of 1916: "There is a steady stream of new arrivals who up to now have been living in either Turkish or Kurdish villages or Turkish homes. Now that living costs are high, they are being sent away without anything... Money is losing so much value that when we receive one lira, which used to be worth 108 piastres it is now only worth 34, and the value is becoming less all the time" (2001, page 168). For an examination of the famine's disastrous impact on those Armenians who had survived until that point, see Vahé Tachjian's *Daily Life in the Abyss*, chapter 4: "Descriptions of the Deportees' Decline: The Deaths of Shoghagat, Hagop, Krikor, Diruhi, and Many Others," pages 128-154 (2019).

203   A teenage girl would have been terrified of walking alone to the city of Mardin. Guleeg Haroian's oral history clarifies the journey was dangerous even for adults in escorted caravans, and scholars note the lawless conditions at that time, for example: "...the Pasha says it is not safe for us to go Mardin now, the road being frequented by wild Arabs" (Harris, 1897, page 87). Onto these lawless roads, the Muslim family cast 14-year-old Mary Haroian, after having used her as unpaid labor for years.

204   Mary would have had to accept conversion to Islam to enter the orphanage in Mardin. Orphanages were "generally poor; they lacked proper food and clothing" and major epidemics such as cholera often "killed many children." One Danish missionary lists the diseases ravaging the country: "There is so much sickness. Typhus, black smallpox, dysentery, pneumonia, measles, and much else" (2001, page 179). The potential for abuse of the children was high in the orphanage's "authoritarian institutional setting" and for those who survived, being an orphan "carried a perpetual stigma" (Sanasarian, 1989, page 456).

205   Mary confided in Eva that she had prayed to God to let her see one face of a loved one so that she could die in peace (Hightaian, Personal Interview).

206   Derderian posits many forced brides would have left had they had living parents (2005, page 13). Eva was fortunate that she had both parents living, including an able-bodied father in the U.S.

207   *Muhajirs* were re-settled Muslim refugees from Russia or parts of Europe that had broken free from the Ottoman Empire, and some were vengeful, inflicting proxy vengeance on the Armenians in the Ottoman Empire. Moreover, Turkish scholar Göçek provides a breathtaking study how Turkey's political leaders channeled the nation's collective emotions into "anger toward weak, unprotected domestic targets like the Armenians, often a proxy for the larger, stronger, and therefore not easily challengeable marks such as Western powers"

(Göçek, 2015, page 36). The Turks began to inflict proxy vengeance on the Armenians increasingly after the Russo-Ottoman War of 1877-8 which "reminded the dominant group that the Ottoman Empire had begun an irreversible decline and was losing its possessions one after another" (Kévorkian, 2011, page 9). The Balkan Wars that brought about the "demise of European Turkey" were yet another source of proxy vengeance inflicted on the Armenians (Kévorkian, 2011, page 141). The political leaders continued to exact "proxy vengeance on unarmed Armenians" for the limited numbers of Armenians fighting with the Russian forces in WWI (Göçek, pages 38, 113, 116-120, 129, 188-191, 228, 246; Kerr, 1973, page 12; Kieser, 2018, page 292; Morris and She'evi, 2019, page 498).

208   The British and French had re-patriated tens of thousands of Armenian refugees from the desert concentration camps to Cilicia, a territory under Allied control, whose capital was Adana. The French brought in Armenian Legionnaires to supplement their own limited troops. Survivors flocked to Allied-occupied territories such as Adana and Constantinople that were safer for them than rural areas or remnant concentration camps (Ekmekcioglu, 2016, page 23).

209   Bedros Haroian identifies some of the Tademtzi who joined this group in *Memoirs of a Soldier About the Days of Tragedy*: "Mambre Tovmasian, Tateos Sahagian, Kachadoor Haroian, and Hovhanes Elloian were not survivors of the genocide. The four had joined the Armenian Voluntary Group in 1915 and travelled to Russian Armenia. Later, they joined the voluntary armies here to fight for the freedom of our nation" (2021, page 216). Kaloosdian provides a short chapter, "Erzinjian: An Uncertain Refuge" on the volunteer units (2015, pages 203-208).

210   Toward the end of her oral history, Eva interrupts when she mentions survivors in the U.S. that Rose, her sister, would have known.

211 Bedros Haroian became a Sergeant Major in the Armenian Legion, an auxiliary unit of the French Foreign Legion that occupied Cilicia. His experiences are recounted in detail in *Memoirs of a Soldier About the Days of Tragedy*.

212 Two scenarios illustrate what could have happened that made Aunt Marnos hide: (1) the Turks were doing one of their roundups of Armenians hiding in Arabic homes, and (2) the Arabs themselves wanted to kill the Armenian women. For example, Akçam notes, "Arab shepherds killed 36 Armenian women there because ... they ate the hay of the animals" (Akçam, 2018, page 221). Mouradian notes that Arab herdsmen killed dozens of women at one concentration camp in the Syrian desert because they were gathering greens by the river, which the Arab herdsmen used to feed their livestock (2021, page 107).

213 The old Turkish *oka* was just over one kilogram (the new *oka* equals one kilogram).

214 Understandable is our urge to think acts of cannibalism are apocryphal, but "Studies indicate that at least a third of the world's cultures have practiced cannibalism associated with warfare or ritual or both," says Washington State University archeologist William Lipe (quote in Roberts, 2003, page 72). Most of those instances took place in the distant past, but not all. For example, the German Buchenwald Concentration Camp contained Jewish skin artifacts, such as a lampshade.

Index

D

E

F

G

H